Why You Behave The Way You Do

Proven Strategies for Lasting Change and Improvement

Trenton H. P. Williams

Why You Behave The Way You Do

TABLE OF CONTENTS

Introduction: The Search for Understanding Human Behavior

Human behaviour is one of the most complex, fascinating, and essential subjects to explore. It influences every aspect of our daily lives, from the decisions we make to the way we interact with others. Understanding why people behave the way they do is not only a matter of curiosity, but it is also crucial for improving personal relationships, advancing in professional settings, and fostering a deeper sense of self-awareness. By gaining insight into behaviour, we can address issues more effectively and lead lives that align better with our goals and values.

Why Understanding Human Behavior is Crucial

At the core of everything we do lies a pattern of behaviour, whether it's conscious or subconscious. These patterns govern how we respond to challenges, interact with others, and approach both opportunities and obstacles. Without understanding the root causes of behaviour, we often find ourselves reacting to situations based on impulse or long-standing habits, sometimes without fully recognizing why.

One of the key reasons why understanding human behaviour is essential is that it allows us to reflect on the "why" behind actions. Why do certain people exhibit patience in stressful situations, while others respond with anger? Why do we sometimes find ourselves repeating the same mistakes, even when we know better? When we pause to analyse and reflect on these behaviours, we uncover valuable insights that help us grow emotionally, mentally, and socially.

Self-awareness is another critical outcome of understanding behaviour. Many of us go through life on autopilot, driven by routines and emotional responses that we rarely question. By examining the reasons behind our choices, we gain greater control over our actions. This kind of reflection can help us break out of unhealthy patterns and replace them with behaviours that serve our personal development.

Additionally, understanding human behaviour allows us to improve our relationships with others. Interpersonal connections, whether familial, romantic, or professional, thrive on understanding and empathy. Misunderstandings, conflicts, and communication breakdowns often stem from not grasping the motivations and emotions driving another person's actions. By taking the time to study behaviour—both our own and others'—we can foster deeper, more meaningful connections and resolve conflicts with greater empathy and insight.

How Our Actions Shape Our Lives and Relationships

Every action we take, no matter how small, plays a role in shaping the trajectory of our lives. Our daily habits, routines, and decisions collectively form the foundation of who we are and how we interact with the world. Whether we are aware of it or not, our behaviour creates ripple effects that extend into all areas of life.

Consider how your actions impact your relationships. For example, consistently showing kindness and understanding to others will likely foster trust and warmth in your personal relationships. On the other hand, reacting with hostility or withdrawing during difficult conversations can strain relationships, sometimes irreparably. Our actions directly affect how others perceive us and, in turn, how they choose to behave toward us.

In professional settings, behaviour also plays a crucial role. How we approach tasks, interact with colleagues, and handle challenges can either lead to growth and success or create obstacles. For instance, an individual who consistently takes initiative, remains open to feedback, and collaborates effectively with others will likely experience career advancement and stronger professional connections. In contrast, someone who avoids responsibility, struggles with communication, or reacts poorly to criticism may find it difficult to progress in their field.

Beyond relationships and professional life, our behaviour also impacts our sense of self and overall well-being. Actions such as regularly engaging in self-care, practising mindfulness, or setting clear boundaries can contribute to mental and emotional health. In contrast, behaviours like procrastination, avoiding difficult tasks, or neglecting our health can lead to stress and dissatisfaction. The decisions we make today, no matter how trivial they may seem, can have long-term effects on our happiness, fulfilment, and success.

Moreover, our behaviours often stem from learned patterns that originate in childhood or early experiences. Many of our adult behaviours are influenced by what we observed growing up—how our parents or caregivers managed conflict, how they expressed love, or how they handled challenges. These learned behaviours often follow us into adulthood and shape our approach to life. While some of these behaviours may serve us well, others may be outdated or unhelpful. Recognizing and addressing these patterns is a key part of personal growth and transformation.

What's particularly important to note is that behaviour is not static—it can be modified and improved over time. By recognizing how our actions shape our present and future, we are empowered to take responsibility for the behaviours that serve us and let go of those that hinder our progress. Behavioural change isn't always easy, but it is possible, especially when we approach it with an open mind and a willingness to reflect on both the positive and negative patterns in our lives.

Understanding human behaviour also provides a framework for making more informed and conscious decisions. When we understand the psychological and emotional drivers behind our actions, we can make choices that are more aligned with our true desires and values. This doesn't just apply to big, life-changing decisions but to everyday interactions and routines. The more we understand about why we behave a certain way, the better equipped we are to make choices that lead to a more fulfilling and meaningful life.

The Foundations of Behaviour: Nature vs. Nurture

The age-old debate surrounding nature versus nurture remains one of the most important questions in understanding human behaviour. At the foundation of who we are as individuals lies the interaction between our biological makeup—our genetics—and the environment in which we are raised. The complex interplay between these two forces shapes not only our personalities but also our actions, tendencies, and reactions to life's challenges. To truly grasp why we behave the way we do, it is essential to explore how both genetics and the environment contribute to our development and daily behaviour.

The Role of Genetics in Shaping Behaviour

Genetics plays a crucial role in forming the biological blueprint of who we are. Every individual inherits a unique combination of genes from their parents, which, in turn, influences physical traits such as height, eye colour, and facial features. However, genetics also extend beyond the visible characteristics of a person to affect temperament, emotional responses, cognitive abilities, and behavioural tendencies.

One of the key ways genetics shape behaviour is through the structure and function of the brain. Different genes can influence how neurotransmitters—chemical messengers in the brain—are produced, processed, and transmitted. For example, serotonin, a neurotransmitter associated with mood regulation, may vary from person to person based on genetic differences. These variations can affect an individual's predisposition to conditions like anxiety, depression, or impulsivity. Similarly, genes involved in the regulation of dopamine, a neurotransmitter linked to motivation and reward, can shape a person's tendency toward risk-taking or pleasure-seeking behaviours.

Beyond neurotransmitters, genetics also influence personality traits. Research on the heritability of personality has shown that some traits are more strongly linked to genetics than others. For instance, traits like extraversion, openness to experience, and neuroticism have been found to have a significant genetic component. Studies involving twins—especially those who were separated at birth and raised in different environments—have provided compelling evidence that genetics play a substantial role in shaping who we are, regardless of upbringing.

However, while genetics provide the framework for many aspects of behaviour, they do not act in isolation. The expression of genes, and the extent to which they influence behaviour, is often modified by environmental factors. This leads to the realisation that while biology sets the stage, the environment plays a critical role in shaping the actual performance.

How Environment and Upbringing Influence Personality and Actions

While genetics offer the blueprint, the environment in which we are raised adds the context that shapes how that blueprint is realised. From birth, individuals are immersed in an environment that includes family, culture, education, social relationships, and external experiences. These factors collectively influence how a person's genetic predispositions are expressed and how they develop over time.

The environment plays an especially significant role during early childhood. It is during these formative years that the foundation of personality and behaviour is built. For example, a child raised in a nurturing and supportive environment is more likely to develop positive social and emotional skills, which contribute to a well-adjusted personality. On the other hand, children exposed to neglect, abuse, or high levels of stress during their upbringing may develop behavioural issues or emotional difficulties that persist into adulthood.

Family dynamics also play a pivotal role in shaping behaviour. Parenting styles—whether authoritarian, permissive, or authoritative—can have a lasting impact on a child's personality and approach to life. For instance, children raised in a supportive and structured environment often develop higher levels of self-esteem and are more likely to succeed academically and socially. In contrast, children raised in chaotic or inconsistent environments may struggle with emotional regulation and form negative coping mechanisms. Even the amount of attention, encouragement, and discipline a child receives influences how they view themselves and interact with the world.

Culture, too, is a significant environmental factor. The societal norms, values, and expectations in which a person is immersed help shape their behaviour and identity. For example, in collectivist cultures where family and community are prioritised, individuals may be more inclined toward cooperative and group-oriented behaviour. In contrast, in individualistic cultures, where personal achievements and independence are highly valued, people may exhibit more competitive and self-focused behaviours. These cultural influences often interact with a person's genetic predispositions, amplifying or modifying certain traits based on the expectations and norms of their environment.

School and peer interactions are also influential during developmental years. Education not only shapes cognitive abilities but also moulds social behaviour. A positive school environment can encourage a child to develop good social skills, learn empathy, and build strong relationships with others. Conversely, exposure to bullying, peer pressure, or rejection can lead to social withdrawal, aggression, or other maladaptive behaviours. The quality of friendships, the influence of teachers, and even extracurricular activities all contribute to a person's behavioural development.

In addition to immediate surroundings, significant life experiences also contribute to shaping behaviour. Traumatic events, such as the loss of a loved one, an accident, or a major life change, can leave lasting imprints on behaviour, often influencing how a person perceives and interacts with the world. The way in which individuals process and cope with these events can either lead to resilience or result in behavioural struggles that affect their daily life.

Examples of How Biology and Experience Interact to Guide Decisions

While genetics and environment each play their part in shaping behaviour, it is the interaction between the two that ultimately determines how a person will behave in a given situation. This dynamic relationship between biology and experience is evident in countless aspects of daily life.

Consider the example of stress response. Some individuals are genetically predisposed to be more sensitive to stress due to their biological makeup—perhaps their nervous system is more reactive, or their body produces higher levels of stress hormones like cortisol. However, whether this predisposition translates into actual stress-related behaviours often depends on the environment. A person raised in a supportive and nurturing environment may learn healthy coping mechanisms, allowing them to manage stress effectively despite their biological sensitivity. In contrast, someone with the same genetic predisposition but raised in a high-stress or unstable environment may develop unhealthy coping strategies, such as avoidance or substance use, to deal with stress.

Another example can be found in the case of intelligence and academic performance. While genetics play a role in determining a person's cognitive abilities, environmental factors such as quality of education, parental involvement, and access to resources are equally important. A child born with a high genetic potential for intelligence may not reach that potential if they are raised in an under-stimulating or neglectful environment. On the other hand, a child with average genetic potential may exceed expectations through exposure to enriching experiences and strong support systems.

Personality traits offer another glimpse into how biology and experience interact. Consider a child born with a genetic predisposition toward introversion. If this child grows up in an environment where they are encouraged to engage in social activities and provided with opportunities to develop social skills, they may learn to navigate social situations comfortably despite their introverted nature. Conversely, if the child is raised in an environment that discourages social interaction or exposes them to negative social experiences, their introverted tendencies may become more pronounced, leading to social anxiety or withdrawal.

Even mental health conditions like anxiety and depression illustrate this interaction. While genetics can increase a person's susceptibility to these conditions, environmental factors such as early life trauma, chronic stress, or lack of social support can trigger or exacerbate symptoms. Conversely, a nurturing and supportive environment can serve as a protective factor, reducing the likelihood that a genetic predisposition will manifest in a full-blown mental health disorder.

Brain Chemistry and Your Behaviour

Human behaviour is deeply influenced by the chemical processes that occur within the brain. Understanding brain chemistry is crucial for comprehending how mood, emotions, and actions are shaped. The brain operates through a delicate balance of neurotransmitters—chemical messengers that facilitate communication between neurons—and hormones that play a vital role in regulating behaviour, emotional responses, and even mental health. By exploring how these chemical interactions function, we can better understand how they influence the way we think, feel, and behave throughout life.

Understanding Neurotransmitters and Their Impact on Mood, Emotions, and Actions

Neurotransmitters are chemicals that transmit signals across synapses from one neuron to another. These signals are responsible for regulating numerous functions, including mood, emotions, and physical actions. The brain uses a wide variety of neurotransmitters, each with its specific function. The balance and availability of these neurotransmitters can significantly impact behaviour, which is why they are often linked to conditions like anxiety, depression, and impulsivity.

One of the most well-known neurotransmitters is **serotonin**, which plays a vital role in regulating mood, sleep, and appetite. Low levels of serotonin have been closely linked to depression, anxiety, and sleep disturbances. People with serotonin imbalances may experience mood swings, irritability, or difficulty managing stress. Medications known as selective serotonin reuptake inhibitors (SSRIs) are commonly prescribed to boost serotonin levels and help stabilise mood in individuals suffering from depression.

Another important neurotransmitter is **dopamine**, often referred to as the brain's "reward chemical." Dopamine regulates feelings of pleasure, motivation, and reward-seeking behaviour. When dopamine levels are high, individuals are more likely to experience a sense of satisfaction and fulfilment. However, when dopamine levels are low, motivation decreases, and feelings of apathy or lack of interest may emerge. Dopamine imbalances have been associated with conditions such as Parkinson's disease, which results in motor control issues, and schizophrenia, which can lead to delusions and hallucinations.

Norepinephrine, another neurotransmitter, is closely tied to the body's "fight or flight" response. It helps to mobilise the body and mind during stressful situations, increasing alertness, focus, and energy levels. However, when norepinephrine levels are consistently elevated due to chronic stress, it can contribute to anxiety, restlessness, and high blood pressure.

Another key neurotransmitter is **gamma-aminobutyric acid (GABA)**, which is primarily responsible for calming the brain and reducing over-excitation. When GABA is functioning properly, it helps to manage anxiety and prevent excessive neural activity. Low GABA levels are often associated with increased anxiety, panic attacks, and other stress-related disorders.

The interaction of neurotransmitters is what allows the brain to regulate mood, cognition, and behaviour effectively. However, when these chemical messengers are imbalanced, disrupted, or depleted, they can have a profound impact on emotional regulation and decision-making. Understanding how neurotransmitters work helps to explain why some individuals are more prone to mood disorders, while others may exhibit behaviours related to addiction, impulsivity, or aggression.

The Connection Between Brain Chemistry and Mental Health

The balance of brain chemistry is crucial to maintaining mental health. When neurotransmitters and hormones are functioning harmoniously, an individual is more likely to experience emotional stability and sound mental health. However, disruptions in brain chemistry can lead to various mental health conditions that affect behaviour, thought processes, and mood regulation.

Depression is one of the most common mental health disorders tied to brain chemistry imbalances. Low levels of serotonin, dopamine, and norepinephrine are often found in individuals with depression. This imbalance can lead to prolonged feelings of sadness, loss of interest in previously enjoyed activities, and difficulty concentrating. Treatment for depression often involves medications that help restore balance by increasing the availability of these neurotransmitters in the brain.

Similarly, **anxiety disorders** are linked to irregularities in neurotransmitters such as GABA and serotonin. Individuals with low GABA activity may experience heightened anxiety, leading to a constant state of nervousness or tension. Chronic anxiety can also trigger overproduction of norepinephrine, intensifying the body's stress response. These imbalances can cause people to react disproportionately to minor stressors, leaving them feeling overwhelmed by everyday challenges.

In conditions like **bipolar disorder**, the brain experiences fluctuations in neurotransmitter levels, particularly serotonin and dopamine. These fluctuations cause mood swings, alternating between depressive episodes and periods of mania or heightened energy. During manic episodes, individuals may feel euphoric, impulsive, or engage in risky behaviours due to the elevated dopamine levels. Managing bipolar disorder often involves mood-stabilising medications that help regulate these extreme shifts in brain chemistry.

Schizophrenia, another severe mental health condition, is thought to be associated with excessive dopamine activity. Individuals with schizophrenia may experience distorted perceptions of reality, delusions, and hallucinations due to overactive dopamine receptors. Medications designed to reduce dopamine activity in specific areas of the brain are commonly used to manage the symptoms of schizophrenia.

By understanding the connection between brain chemistry and mental health, we can appreciate the importance of maintaining chemical balance within the brain. For many individuals, mental health issues arise when there is a disruption in this balance, whether through genetic predisposition, environmental stress, or substance abuse. In some cases, psychotherapy, medication, or lifestyle changes can help restore equilibrium and improve mental health.

How Hormonal Changes Can Influence Behavior Throughout Life

Hormones are another critical component of brain chemistry that significantly influences behaviour. Unlike neurotransmitters, which transmit signals directly between neurons, hormones are chemical messengers that are released into the bloodstream and affect various parts of the body, including the brain. Throughout life, hormonal changes can lead to shifts in behaviour, mood, and cognitive function.

During **adolescence**, hormonal changes related to puberty can have a profound impact on behaviour. The surge of hormones such as testosterone in boys and oestrogen in girls contributes to the development of secondary sexual characteristics, but it also affects emotional and behavioural regulation. Adolescents may experience heightened emotions, increased impulsivity, and risk-taking behaviours due to the hormonal fluctuations associated with puberty. These hormonal changes are also linked to the emotional volatility often seen during this stage of development.

Pregnancy and **parenthood** also involve significant hormonal changes that influence behaviour. During pregnancy, hormonal shifts, particularly in oestrogen and progesterone levels, can lead to mood swings, anxiety, or irritability. After childbirth, some individuals experience **postpartum depression**, a condition linked to the dramatic drop in hormone levels that occurs after delivery. The balance of hormones such as oxytocin—often referred to as the "bonding hormone"—plays a vital role in fostering attachment between parents and their newborns, promoting nurturing behaviours and emotional connection.

As individuals age, **menopause** in women and **andropause** in men introduce further hormonal changes that can affect behaviour. Menopause, characterised by a decline in oestrogen and progesterone, often leads to mood swings, irritability, and changes in cognitive function. In men, declining testosterone levels during andropause can result in reduced energy levels, mood changes, and a decrease in motivation or interest in activities that were once enjoyed.

Stress is another factor that triggers hormonal changes, with cortisol being one of the primary stress hormones. In the short term, cortisol helps the body respond to stress by increasing alertness and energy. However, chronic stress leads to prolonged elevated cortisol levels, which can negatively impact behaviour, leading to anxiety, irritability, and cognitive difficulties such as memory loss. Chronic high cortisol levels are also associated with physical health problems like high blood pressure and a weakened immune system.

Understanding how hormones influence behaviour throughout life helps explain many of the changes in mood, motivation, and cognitive function that individuals experience. Whether through adolescence, pregnancy, ageing, or stress, the fluctuations in hormonal levels have a direct impact on brain chemistry and, by extension, on behaviour.

The Role of Cognitive Processes in Shaping Actions

Cognitive processes are central to how we navigate our daily lives, make decisions, and respond to challenges. These processes encompass the ways in which we think, interpret information, and ultimately choose to act. Our thoughts, beliefs, and perceptions have a direct influence on our actions, whether we are conscious of it or not. Understanding the intricate relationship between cognition and behaviour can offer valuable insights into why we act the way we do and how our mental frameworks shape both positive and negative behavioural patterns.

How Thoughts, Beliefs, and Perceptions Influence Decisions

At the core of human behaviour is the concept that our thoughts heavily dictate our actions. Cognitive psychology suggests that the way we interpret and perceive the world around us directly impacts our decisions and, by extension, our behaviour. This cognitive-behavioural link means that much of what we do stems from how we think and how we frame situations mentally.

For example, an individual who believes they are capable and competent will approach challenges with confidence and persistence. Their belief in their own abilities shapes their actions—whether it's taking on new tasks, problem-solving, or pursuing opportunities. On the other hand, someone who holds the belief that they are destined to fail may avoid challenges altogether or give up easily when faced with adversity. This avoidance is not because they lack the skills to succeed, but because their thoughts have already determined their outcome.

Our perceptions of others also play a significant role in shaping our behaviour. Social psychologists have shown that our actions toward others are largely influenced by our perceptions of their intentions, character, and competence. If we perceive someone as trustworthy and kind, we are more likely to engage in cooperative or helping behaviour. Conversely, if we perceive someone as untrustworthy or selfish, we may act defensively or with suspicion, even if their actual behaviour does not warrant such a response.

Another important cognitive factor influencing behaviour is **self-talk**—the internal dialogue we maintain with ourselves. Positive self-talk, which is characterised by encouraging and constructive thoughts, can lead to higher motivation, resilience, and the willingness to take risks. Negative self-talk, on the other hand, fosters doubt, fear, and hesitation, often resulting in inaction or avoidance of challenges. This internal dialogue is shaped by past experiences, cultural conditioning, and personal beliefs, all of which create a filter through which we view our capabilities and opportunities.

Perceptions of control, known as **locus of control**, further illustrate how cognitive processes shape behaviour. Individuals with an internal locus of control believe that their actions directly influence outcomes, leading them to take responsibility for their behaviour and work toward desired goals. In contrast, those with an external locus of control believe that outcomes are determined by external forces beyond their control, often resulting in feelings of helplessness and a tendency to blame others or circumstances for their failures.

The Psychology of Automatic vs. Deliberate Behaviours

Human behaviour can generally be categorised into two types: automatic behaviours and deliberate behaviours. These two modes of action represent different cognitive pathways that guide how we respond to situations and make decisions.

Automatic behaviours are those actions that occur without conscious thought or effort. These behaviours are often habitual, formed through repeated experiences and practice. Over time, certain actions become so routine that they no longer require active cognitive engagement. For example, when driving a familiar route or brushing your teeth, you don't actively think about each step—you simply do it. These automatic behaviours are efficient because they free up cognitive resources for more complex tasks. However, they can also be problematic when negative habits or reflexive reactions dominate without critical reflection.

One of the key elements of automatic behaviour is **heuristics**—mental shortcuts or rules of thumb that allow us to make quick judgments. While heuristics can be useful in decision-making, they can also lead to cognitive biases, where we make errors in judgement based on faulty or oversimplified reasoning. For example, the **availability heuristic** leads people to overestimate the likelihood of events based on how easily examples come to mind. This is why people may fear rare events, such as plane crashes, more than common risks like car accidents.

On the other hand, **deliberate behaviours** involve conscious thought, effort, and decision-making. These actions occur when we intentionally evaluate our options, weigh the consequences, and choose the best course of action. Deliberate behaviours are often required for solving complex problems, making important life decisions, or navigating unfamiliar situations. For instance, when deciding whether to accept a new job offer or enter a significant relationship, individuals are more likely to engage in deliberate behaviours that involve careful consideration of various factors.

The **dual-process theory** of cognition explains the difference between these two types of behaviour. According to this theory, human thought operates on two levels: **System 1**, which is fast, automatic, and emotional, and **System 2**, which is slow, deliberate, and logical. While System 1 is responsible for everyday automatic actions, System 2 is engaged when we face novel or challenging situations that require thoughtful analysis.

However, the interaction between automatic and deliberate behaviour is not always straightforward. At times, habits or automatic responses can override rational decision-making, leading to impulsive or counterproductive behaviour. For example, someone who has developed the automatic habit of snacking when stressed may find it difficult to stop, even when they consciously recognize that it's unhealthy. Similarly, individuals prone to anger may react automatically in frustrating situations, without pausing to reflect on the potential consequences of their outburst.

How Cognitive Distortions Lead to Negative Behavior Patterns

Cognitive distortions are biassed ways of thinking that reinforce negative beliefs and behaviours. These distortions often lead to irrational or exaggerated perceptions of reality, causing individuals to act in ways that are not aligned with their best interests. Understanding cognitive distortions can help us recognize how flawed thinking patterns contribute to negative behaviour cycles.

One common cognitive distortion is **all-or-nothing thinking**, where individuals view situations in black-and-white terms. This type of thinking leads people to believe that outcomes are either completely successful or complete failures, with no room for nuance. For example, a student who receives a lower grade on one assignment may conclude that they are a total failure, even though their overall academic performance may be strong. This distorted thinking often results in perfectionism, procrastination, and avoidance, as individuals fear not meeting their high standards.

Catastrophizing is another cognitive distortion that leads to exaggerated negative thinking. Individuals who catastrophize tend to expect the worst possible outcome in any given situation, even when the likelihood of such an outcome is low. For example, someone who experiences a minor disagreement with a coworker might assume that it will lead to job loss or social isolation. This distorted thinking pattern can trigger anxiety, stress, and avoidance behaviours, as individuals feel overwhelmed by imagined worst-case scenarios.

Overgeneralization occurs when individuals take a single negative experience and apply it broadly to their entire life. For instance, if someone is rejected after asking a person on a date, they might conclude that they are unlovable or destined to be alone forever. This distorted way of thinking perpetuates a cycle of low self-esteem and self-sabotaging behaviours, as individuals internalise negative outcomes and believe that they will inevitably recur.

Mind reading is another distortion that involves assuming we know what others are thinking, often to our detriment. For example, a person might believe that others think poorly of them, even in the absence of evidence. This belief can lead to social withdrawal, defensive behaviour, or excessive people-pleasing as individuals try to avoid the negative judgments they imagine others are making. In reality, these assumptions are often unfounded, but they influence behaviour in significant ways.

Breaking free from cognitive distortions requires individuals to challenge their automatic negative thoughts and replace them with more rational, evidence-based thinking. Cognitive-behavioural therapy (CBT) is a widely used approach to help people recognize and reframe distorted thought patterns. By identifying the underlying beliefs driving negative behaviours, individuals can gain greater control over their actions and develop healthier coping strategies.

The Influence of Emotions on Decision-Making

Human decision-making is rarely as logical and rational as we might like to believe. While logic and reason play important roles in how we choose to act, our emotions are often the driving force behind many of our decisions. Emotions provide a framework for how we perceive situations and evaluate options. Understanding the profound influence of emotions on decision-making is key to better managing our actions, especially in high-stakes or stressful scenarios.

The Power of Emotions and Their Impact on Rational Thinking

Emotions are powerful motivators, and their effect on decision-making is often immediate and profound. They influence how we process information, assess risks, and prioritise goals. While logical reasoning is supposed to guide our decisions, emotions frequently take the lead, shaping our perceptions and pushing us toward choices that may not always align with reasoned thinking.

For instance, when individuals feel strongly about a situation, they are likely to make snap judgments based on their emotional state rather than carefully weighing the facts. Someone experiencing intense anger may react aggressively in a conflict, without taking the time to consider the long-term consequences of their actions. Similarly, a person feeling overjoyed might commit to something impulsively, such as making a large purchase, without considering its practicality.

One of the key reasons emotions have such a strong influence on decision-making is that they operate in a faster and more primal part of the brain than logic. The emotional centres of the brain, particularly the **amygdala**, are responsible for processing and responding to emotional stimuli quickly. This rapid response can be beneficial in situations requiring immediate action, such as escaping a threat. However, in complex decisions where careful thought is needed, emotions can sometimes cloud judgement and lead to poor choices.

Moreover, emotions tend to colour the way we interpret the information around us. This cognitive bias, known as **emotional reasoning**, occurs when we assume that because we feel a certain way, it must reflect reality. For example, if someone feels anxious about a social gathering, they might conclude that the event will be uncomfortable or unpleasant, even if there is no evidence to support this assumption. Emotional reasoning can lead people to avoid situations unnecessarily, as they allow their emotions to dominate their decision-making process rather than objectively evaluating the facts.

How Fear, Anger, Happiness, and Sadness Affect Choices and Actions

Different emotions uniquely influence the decisions we make, often in ways that are deeply tied to their evolutionary roots. Understanding the distinct effects of common emotions such as fear, anger, happiness, and sadness can provide insight into how emotions shape behaviour in various contexts.

Fear, for example, is a powerful emotion that can drive decision-making by triggering the body's natural fight-or-flight response. When faced with a perceived threat, fear encourages us to act quickly, either by avoiding danger or confronting it head-on. While this reaction can be life-saving in certain situations, fear can also lead to overly cautious or irrational decisions in non-threatening contexts. For instance, fear of failure may cause someone to avoid taking risks, even when those risks are necessary for personal growth. Fear can also lead to **risk aversion**, where individuals choose the safest option to avoid potential negative outcomes, even if the more challenging option could lead to greater rewards.

Anger is another emotion that significantly influences decision-making, often by leading to impulsive and sometimes destructive actions. When people are angry, they are more likely to act without fully considering the consequences, as anger narrows their focus and heightens their desire for immediate resolution. For example, in moments of anger, individuals might say hurtful things or make rash decisions that they later regret. Research has shown that anger can also increase individuals' confidence in their decisions, even when those decisions are irrational. This overconfidence can result in poor choices that are difficult to reverse, such as quitting a job abruptly or ending a relationship without fully thinking it through.

On the opposite end of the spectrum, **happiness** can also sway decision-making, often leading to more optimistic and risk-taking behaviour. When people feel happy, they tend to view situations more positively and are more likely to engage in behaviours that reflect their elevated mood. For instance, individuals in a happy state may be more open to trying new experiences or making bold investments, as they feel more confident about the potential for success. However, this optimism can sometimes lead to overlooking potential risks or downsides, as the desire to maintain positive feelings can cloud objective judgement.

Sadness, on the other hand, tends to have a dampening effect on decision-making. When people are sad, they may become more reflective and cautious, leading to slower and more deliberate decision-making processes. However, sadness can also contribute to indecision or a lack of motivation, as individuals may feel overwhelmed by their emotions and struggle to take action. In some cases, sadness may cause people to seek comfort through familiar routines or avoid new challenges altogether, as they prioritise emotional stability over taking risks.

Emotional Triggers That Often Lead to Impulsive Behaviours

Impulsive behaviours are often driven by strong emotional triggers, which can override the brain's capacity for self-regulation and rational thought. These emotional triggers, whether rooted in anger, fear, excitement, or frustration, can prompt individuals to act without fully considering the consequences.

One common emotional trigger for impulsive behaviour is **stress**. When individuals are under stress, their ability to think clearly and rationally diminishes. Stress activates the **sympathetic nervous system**, causing the release of hormones such as cortisol and adrenaline. These hormones prepare the body for immediate action, but they also reduce the brain's capacity for long-term planning and decision-making. As a result, people under stress may act impulsively—whether it's making an unplanned purchase, lashing out at a loved one, or quitting a job—without considering the potential long-term impact of their actions.

Frustration is another emotional trigger that often leads to impulsive behaviour. When people experience frustration, especially if it stems from unmet expectations or obstacles in their way, they may feel compelled to act quickly to relieve the negative emotion. For example, someone who is frustrated by slow progress in a project might abandon it altogether in a moment of impatience, even if they were close to achieving their goal. Similarly, frustration in a relationship can lead to impulsive actions such as arguing, walking away, or making decisions without proper communication.

Excitement and **anticipation** are also strong emotional triggers that can prompt impulsive decisions. The thrill of a new opportunity or the excitement of a potential reward can cause people to overlook risks and act on impulse. For instance, the excitement of winning a game or receiving a bonus may lead someone to make a hasty purchase or investment without fully evaluating the consequences. This kind of impulsive behaviour is often driven by a desire for instant gratification, as the emotional high of the moment takes precedence over careful consideration of long-term outcomes.

Even **boredom** can be an emotional trigger for impulsive behaviour. When individuals feel bored, they may seek out stimulation or excitement to alleviate the discomfort of inactivity. This can lead to spontaneous decisions that prioritise short-term pleasure over long-term planning, such as engaging in risky behaviours or making unnecessary purchases. The need to escape boredom can push people toward decisions that they might later regret, as the choices made in such moments are often reactive rather than thoughtful.

Social Influences and Behavioural Norms

Human behaviour is rarely an entirely individual phenomenon. It is shaped not only by personal beliefs and values but also by a broad range of social factors that exert subtle yet powerful influences. Societal expectations, peer groups, family dynamics, cultural traditions, and media all contribute to defining what is considered acceptable or "normal" behaviour.

Understanding these social influences provides insight into why people act the way they do and how their actions are often guided by the need to conform to external standards, sometimes even at the expense of personal desires or beliefs.

The Effect of Societal Expectations on Behavior

Societal expectations form an invisible framework within which people navigate their lives. These expectations dictate how individuals should behave, communicate, dress, and even think in different settings. From early childhood, people are taught what is considered appropriate behaviour in various situations, whether in school, work, or public spaces. These societal standards influence behaviour by reinforcing the idea that deviation from the norm may lead to social disapproval or rejection.

One of the most potent ways societal expectations shape behaviour is through the concept of **social roles**. Each person occupies multiple roles in society—such as being a parent, employee, student, or friend—and each role comes with its own set of behavioural norms. For example, society expects teachers to act with authority and professionalism in the classroom, while also showing compassion and patience toward students. Similarly, society expects parents to be nurturing and responsible, guiding their children with love and discipline.

When people fulfil these social roles, they often do so out of a sense of obligation or responsibility, even if their personal desires or emotions might lead them in a different direction. A parent might sacrifice personal interests or hobbies to spend more time with their children because society upholds this as the "right" thing to do. At times, the pressure to meet these expectations can cause stress, particularly when personal beliefs or circumstances conflict with societal standards. For instance, someone may feel pressured to stay in a job they dislike simply because society equates professional success with stability and status.

In many cultures, societal expectations around gender roles have historically been especially rigid. Men were traditionally expected to be the providers and protectors, while women were expected to be caregivers and homemakers.

While these roles have evolved, they still influence behaviour, often creating internal conflicts for individuals who do not identify with these traditional roles. A woman pursuing a career in a male-dominated field might face societal pressure to conform to traditional gender norms, while a man choosing to stay home to raise his children might be questioned for stepping outside of the typical male role.

How Peer Pressure and Social Conformity Shape Actions

Peer pressure is one of the most direct forms of social influence, particularly during adolescence and early adulthood, though it continues to exert its effects throughout life. It occurs when individuals feel compelled to conform to the behaviours, attitudes, or choices of a group in order to gain acceptance or avoid social rejection. Peer pressure can be positive, encouraging individuals to engage in beneficial activities such as studying hard or participating in community service, but it can also lead to negative behaviours such as substance abuse, reckless actions, or unhealthy competition.

Social conformity, closely related to peer pressure, refers to the tendency to adjust one's behaviour to align with group norms. This desire to conform is often driven by the human need to belong, as being part of a group provides emotional support, security, and identity. In many situations, people conform to avoid being labelled as different or outcast, even when their personal preferences might not align with the group's behaviours or beliefs.

One classic example of social conformity is **Asch's conformity experiments**, where participants were asked to provide answers to simple questions in a group setting. Despite knowing the correct answers, many participants conformed to the incorrect responses given by the majority, demonstrating the powerful effect of group influence. This experiment highlights how individuals may prioritise group harmony and acceptance over personal accuracy or authenticity.

In everyday life, social conformity can manifest in decisions as small as fashion choices or as significant as political or religious affiliations. Someone might wear a particular brand of clothing not because they personally prefer it but because their peer group favours it, or they might adopt the political opinions of their friends and family even if they don't fully agree. This tendency to conform becomes particularly evident in environments such as schools, workplaces, or social media, where visible differences from group norms can lead to social exclusion or ridicule.

Social media platforms, in particular, amplify peer pressure and social conformity by creating environments where individuals' actions are constantly visible and subject to scrutiny. The desire to gain "likes," followers, or social validation can influence people to behave in ways that align with popular trends, sometimes at the cost of their personal values. For example, someone might post content they don't fully support or take part in viral challenges simply to feel included in the broader social conversation.

The Role of Family, Culture, and Media in Defining "Normal" Behavior

Family, culture, and media are powerful agents of socialisation that help shape people's understanding of what is "normal" behaviour. From birth, individuals are influenced by these forces, which provide them with the values, beliefs, and behaviours they will carry into adulthood.

Family plays a foundational role in shaping behaviour. Children learn their earliest lessons about acceptable behaviour from parents and other family members, who model and reinforce certain actions. Through direct instruction and observation, individuals internalise family values, traditions, and rules that guide their behaviour throughout life. For instance, a family that emphasises the importance of education is likely to raise children who value academic achievement and pursue higher learning. Conversely, a family that prioritises independence and self-reliance might raise children who are more inclined to take risks or seek out entrepreneurial paths.

Family dynamics also influence how individuals behave in relationships. For example, people who grew up in homes where communication was open and supportive are more likely to engage in healthy communication in their own relationships. On the other hand, individuals who experienced conflict or dysfunction in their families may struggle with forming healthy boundaries or managing conflict later in life.

Culture further expands the scope of influence by providing the broader social context in which individuals live. Cultural norms vary widely across societies and dictate behaviour in areas such as morality, gender roles, religious practices, and communication styles. For example, some cultures emphasise collective responsibility and prioritise group harmony over individual desires, while others promote individualism and personal autonomy. These cultural values significantly shape behaviour by setting expectations for how people should interact with others and make decisions in daily life.

Cultural norms also dictate how people respond to challenges, successes, and failures. In cultures that value emotional restraint, individuals might suppress their feelings in public, even in situations of extreme distress. Meanwhile, cultures that encourage emotional expression may see open displays of emotions as not only acceptable but necessary for social bonding. These cultural variations highlight how behaviour is often a reflection of the broader societal context, rather than purely individual choice.

Media, especially in the digital age, plays a crucial role in shaping perceptions of normal behaviour. Television, movies, social media, and news outlets create powerful narratives about how people should look, act, and interact. Media representations often shape societal standards, influencing how individuals perceive themselves and others. For instance, repeated exposure to media portrayals of certain body types, success stories, or lifestyles can create pressure to conform to those ideals, even if they are unrealistic or unattainable.

The rise of social media platforms has heightened this influence, as individuals are constantly exposed to curated versions of other people's lives. This exposure can create unrealistic expectations of success, beauty, and happiness, leading individuals to engage in behaviours aimed at fitting into these socially constructed ideals. The pressure to conform to media-driven standards can affect self-esteem, mental health, and personal decision-making, as people compare themselves to the often idealised images and lifestyles presented by influencers and celebrities.

Personality Types and Behavioural Tendencies

Understanding human behaviour requires an examination of personality, a fundamental aspect that predicts how individuals are likely to act in various situations. Personality encompasses the consistent patterns of thinking, feeling, and behaving that make people unique. While external influences like environment and social norms play a role in shaping behaviour, the internal world of personality traits has a significant impact on how individuals respond to those influences. By understanding personality traits and models, we can gain deeper insight into how different individuals approach decisions, manage relationships, and navigate life's challenges.

How Personality Traits Predict Behaviour

Personality traits serve as predictors for how people behave in different circumstances. These traits are enduring characteristics that remain relatively stable over time and across situations. For instance, a person who is generally agreeable is likely to be cooperative, kind, and empathetic not only at work but also in social and family settings. Conversely, someone with high levels of neuroticism may frequently experience anxiety, irritability, or emotional instability, influencing how they handle stress or conflicts in daily life.

One way to understand the connection between personality traits and behaviour is through **dispositional theory**, which suggests that individuals' behaviours are largely driven by their inherent traits. For example, someone who is high in conscientiousness is likely to be organised, responsible, and detail-oriented, which can lead to success in careers that require planning and precision, such as project management or engineering. On the other hand, a person who scores low in conscientiousness might struggle with deadlines, overlook details, or be less reliable in professional or personal commitments.

In the same vein, traits like **extraversion** or **introversion** influence how individuals interact with others. Extroverts, who are typically sociable and energetic, may thrive in settings that involve teamwork, public speaking, or leadership roles. Introverts, who tend to prefer solitary or low-stimulation environments, might gravitate toward professions that allow for deep focus and independent work, such as writing, research, or design. These traits don't just influence career choices but also impact social relationships, decision-making processes, and how individuals handle stress or conflict.

While personality traits are powerful predictors of behaviour, it's important to note that they do not dictate behaviour in every situation. Context, emotional state, and external pressures can modify how a trait is expressed. For instance, even a highly conscientious person might occasionally miss a deadline due to unforeseen circumstances. However, over the long term, personality traits provide a reliable framework for predicting behavioural tendencies.

The Different Personality Models and What They Mean for Your Actions

Several models have been developed to categorise and understand personality traits, but one of the most widely accepted frameworks is the **Big Five Personality Traits** model. This model identifies five core dimensions of personality: Openness to Experience, Conscientiousness, Extraversion, Agreeableness, and Neuroticism (often remembered by the acronym OCEAN). These traits encompass a broad range of behaviours and attitudes that collectively shape an individual's personality.

1. **Openness to Experience**: Individuals high in this trait are often curious, imaginative, and open to new ideas and experiences. They enjoy exploring novel concepts and are more likely to take risks in pursuit of learning or adventure. In contrast, those who score low in openness may prefer routine, familiarity, and practical solutions, often avoiding uncertainty or unconventional ideas. This trait influences behaviour in areas such as career choices, hobbies, and decision-making. A person high in openness may seek out creative or exploratory professions, while someone low in openness may prefer stable, predictable work environments.

2. **Conscientiousness**: People with high levels of conscientiousness are often diligent, organised, and responsible. They tend to set goals, follow through with plans, and exhibit a strong sense of duty. This trait is a strong predictor of academic and career success, as conscientious

individuals are more likely to meet deadlines, maintain focus, and manage tasks efficiently. Low conscientiousness, on the other hand, may result in procrastination, disorganisation, and a lack of attention to detail. Highly conscientious individuals are more likely to engage in behaviours that promote long-term success, such as saving money, maintaining healthy routines, or building strong work habits.

3. **Extraversion**: This trait reflects how individuals interact with the external world. Extroverts are energised by social interactions, enjoy being the centre of attention, and tend to be outgoing and assertive. Introverts, by contrast, are more reserved and may find social interactions draining, often preferring solitude or small, intimate gatherings. Extraversion influences how individuals approach relationships, social gatherings, and professional networking. While extroverts might seek out group activities and thrive

in leadership positions, introverts may excel in roles that allow for independent thought and reflection.

4. **Agreeableness**: High levels of agreeableness are associated with compassion, empathy, and cooperation. Agreeable individuals are often trusting, altruistic, and motivated by the desire to help others. They tend to avoid conflict and seek harmony in relationships. Those who score low on agreeableness might be more competitive, sceptical, or focused on their own needs. This trait has a significant impact on social relationships and teamwork. Highly agreeable people are often good collaborators, but may struggle to assert themselves in competitive environments, while less agreeable individuals may excel in roles that require negotiation or assertiveness.

5. **Neuroticism**: Neuroticism reflects emotional instability and the tendency to experience negative emotions such as anxiety, anger, or sadness. People high in

neuroticism may have difficulty coping with stress and are more prone to mood swings and emotional reactivity. Those low in neuroticism are typically more emotionally stable and better equipped to handle stress. This trait is closely linked to mental health, as high neuroticism can increase the likelihood of experiencing anxiety disorders or depression. In terms of behaviour, individuals high in neuroticism may react more strongly to perceived threats or challenges, while those low in neuroticism are more likely to remain calm and collected under pressure.

Each of these traits contributes to a person's overall personality profile, and their interaction helps to predict behaviour across different settings. The Big Five model is particularly useful because it captures a wide range of behaviours and allows for a nuanced understanding of how personality influences actions.

How Introverts and Extroverts Approach Decisions Differently

The difference between introverts and extroverts is one of the most well-known distinctions in personality psychology, and it has profound implications for how individuals make decisions. Extroverts, who gain energy from social interactions and external stimuli, are often quick to act, driven by a desire for immediate feedback or reward. Introverts, on the other hand, tend to be more reflective, taking time to consider their options before making a decision.

Extroverts tend to approach decisions with confidence and enthusiasm. They often seek out opportunities that involve collaboration, teamwork, and social engagement. In decision-making, extroverts may prioritise quick, actionable results and are more likely to take risks, particularly if the decision involves social or financial rewards. Their natural inclination to engage with others means they are more comfortable seeking advice or input from a wide range of sources before making a choice. However, this can sometimes lead to impulsive decisions, especially in high-stakes situations where extroverts may prioritise action over careful reflection.

Introverts, by contrast, are more likely to approach decisions methodically and with caution. They prefer to gather information and consider all possible outcomes before acting, often relying on their own internal judgement rather than seeking external validation. This careful, deliberate approach means that introverts are less likely to make impulsive decisions and are generally more thoughtful in considering long-term consequences. However, this tendency to overanalyze can sometimes lead to indecision or hesitation, particularly in fast-paced environments where quick decisions are required.

The differences in how introverts and extroverts approach decision-making can be particularly noticeable in professional settings. Extroverts often excel in leadership roles that require quick thinking, decisive action, and public speaking, while introverts may thrive in roles that involve deep focus, critical analysis, or creative problem-solving. In group decision-making scenarios, extroverts may dominate discussions, while introverts may prefer to contribute through written feedback or after private reflection.

Despite these differences, both introverts and extroverts can be equally effective decision-makers. Introverts' thoughtful, cautious approach can lead to well-considered, strategic decisions, while extroverts' energy and assertiveness can drive swift, decisive action in situations that demand it. Understanding these tendencies allows individuals to better navigate their strengths and weaknesses in decision-making processes and can also foster more effective collaboration between introverts and extroverts in team settings.

The Subconscious Mind and Its Role in Daily Actions

The human mind is a complex system, with only a small portion of its processes happening at the conscious level. A significant amount of our behaviour, decisions, and reactions are actually shaped by the subconscious. The subconscious mind operates continuously in the background, storing memories, emotions, and learned behaviours that influence our daily actions without us being fully aware of them. Understanding the role of the subconscious mind is crucial to gaining better control over one's behaviour, as well as unlocking the power of self-awareness and personal growth.

How Much of Our Behavior Is Driven by Subconscious Influences

A large part of our daily behaviour is influenced by subconscious patterns. The subconscious mind serves as a vast storage system for our memories, beliefs, habits, and emotional responses. Unlike the conscious mind, which deals with active thinking and decision-making, the subconscious mind operates automatically, guiding many of our actions based on past experiences and learned behaviours. Studies in psychology suggest that up to 95% of our behaviours are driven by subconscious processes, meaning that much of what we do each day happens without our conscious awareness.

For example, when we brush our teeth, drive a familiar route, or follow a daily routine, we often perform these actions without actively thinking about them. These automatic behaviours are the result of subconscious learning and repetition. Over time, the brain creates neural pathways that allow these actions to become habitual, requiring little to no conscious effort. This is an efficient way for the brain to conserve energy, as it frees up mental resources for more complex tasks.

However, subconscious influences go beyond mere routines. Our emotional responses, preferences, and biases are also largely shaped by the subconscious mind. For instance, we may find ourselves instantly liking or disliking certain people or situations without fully understanding why. These reactions often stem from past experiences or ingrained beliefs stored in the subconscious. Similarly, our fears and anxieties are often rooted in subconscious memories or unresolved emotional issues, which can trigger responses long after the original event has passed.

The Impact of Past Experiences and Traumas Stored in the Subconscious

The subconscious mind plays a key role in storing past experiences, including both positive and negative events. While pleasant memories can lead to constructive behaviours and emotional well-being, unresolved trauma or negative experiences can have lasting effects on a person's behaviour and mental health. Traumas, particularly those experienced in childhood, can become deeply embedded in the subconscious mind and influence actions for years or even decades later.

For example, someone who experienced neglect or emotional abuse during childhood may develop subconscious beliefs about their worthiness or ability to form healthy relationships. These beliefs can manifest in adult life as self-sabotaging behaviours, such as avoiding intimacy or pushing people away, without the individual fully understanding the underlying cause. Similarly, traumatic experiences such as accidents, bullying, or loss can trigger subconscious defence mechanisms, leading to anxiety, hypervigilance, or avoidance of certain situations.

The subconscious mind also influences how we interpret new experiences. If someone has experienced repeated failures, their subconscious mind may develop a pattern of expecting failure in future endeavours. This can create a self-fulfilling prophecy, where the fear of failure leads to hesitation, lack of effort, or giving up too soon, reinforcing the belief that success is out of reach. Similarly, individuals who have experienced betrayal or hurt in past relationships may unconsciously expect the same outcome in future relationships, leading to trust issues or avoidance of emotional vulnerability.

Because the subconscious mind does not distinguish between past and present, these stored emotions and beliefs continue to shape our behaviour long after the original events have occurred. The mind often relies on past experiences as a guide for interpreting current situations, which is why unresolved trauma can have such a profound impact on daily actions.

Techniques to Become More Aware of and Control Subconscious Behaviours

While much of the subconscious mind operates automatically, it is possible to become more aware of and gain control over subconscious behaviours. By bringing subconscious patterns to the surface and addressing them consciously, individuals can break free from negative behaviours and foster healthier, more constructive habits. There are several techniques that can help in this process:

1. **Mindfulness and Self-Reflection**: Mindfulness involves paying close attention to thoughts, feelings, and actions in the present moment without judgement. By practising mindfulness, individuals can become more aware of their automatic reactions and subconscious patterns. Regular self-reflection, whether through journaling or meditation, allows individuals to explore the motivations

behind their actions and identify any recurring thoughts or behaviours that may be rooted in the subconscious. This heightened awareness is the first step in changing subconscious behaviours.

2. **Cognitive Behavioral Therapy (CBT)**: CBT is a therapeutic approach that helps individuals identify and change negative thought patterns that influence behaviour. Many of these thought patterns are rooted in the subconscious, such as beliefs about self-worth or fears of failure. Through CBT, individuals can challenge these automatic thoughts and replace them with more realistic, constructive beliefs. This process helps to rewire the brain and create new neural pathways, breaking free from harmful subconscious patterns.

3. **Hypnotherapy**: Hypnotherapy is a technique that involves guiding individuals into a relaxed, trance-like state where they can access their subconscious mind more easily. In this state, the subconscious mind is more receptive to

positive suggestions, allowing individuals to address deep-seated issues such as trauma, phobias, or self-destructive behaviours. Hypnotherapy can be particularly useful for individuals who have difficulty accessing their subconscious beliefs through conscious thought alone.

4. **Visualisation and Affirmations**: Visualisation is a powerful tool for influencing the subconscious mind. By mentally rehearsing positive outcomes or desired behaviours, individuals can program their subconscious to expect success, confidence, or other constructive emotions. Affirmations, which are positive statements repeated regularly, can also help to reprogram negative beliefs stored in the subconscious. For example, repeating affirmations such as "I am worthy of love" or "I am capable of achieving my goals" can gradually reshape subconscious beliefs and

influence behaviour in a positive direction.

5. **Reprocessing Past Trauma**: Addressing past trauma is essential for breaking free from its influence on the subconscious mind. Techniques such as Eye Movement Desensitization and Reprocessing (EMDR) therapy can help individuals process traumatic memories and reduce their emotional impact. By reprocessing these memories in a safe, therapeutic environment, individuals can release the emotional hold that past traumas have on their subconscious and regain control over their behaviour.

6. **Changing Habits**: Since many of our daily actions are driven by subconscious habits, changing those habits can have a profound impact on behaviour. To break free from negative habits, individuals must consciously identify the triggers that lead to those behaviours and replace them with positive alternatives. For instance, someone who subconsciously turns to

unhealthy snacks when stressed can develop a habit of taking a walk or practising deep breathing instead. Over time, the new habit becomes ingrained in the subconscious, replacing the old pattern.

Coping Mechanisms and Their Impact on Behavior

Coping mechanisms are the methods individuals use to manage stress, anxiety, trauma, or difficult emotions. These strategies play a significant role in how people respond to life's challenges, affecting both short-term actions and long-term behavioural patterns. Understanding the difference between healthy and unhealthy coping mechanisms, as well as recognizing the influence of emotional regulation and self-awareness, is essential for managing stress in constructive ways.

Understanding Healthy vs. Unhealthy Coping Strategies

Coping strategies can be broadly divided into two categories: healthy (adaptive) and unhealthy (maladaptive). The effectiveness of a coping mechanism depends on how well it helps the individual reduce stress or manage emotions without causing additional harm to themselves or others.

Healthy coping strategies promote emotional well-being and long-term resilience. These methods help individuals process emotions constructively, solve problems, and maintain mental and physical health. Examples of healthy coping strategies include:

- **Exercise**: Physical activity is a well-known stress reliever that helps reduce anxiety, improve mood, and boost overall health. Exercise releases endorphins, chemicals in the brain that naturally elevate mood and combat stress.

- **Talking to a friend or therapist**: Sharing emotions and experiences with a trusted person can provide emotional relief and valuable perspective. It also allows individuals to receive support and advice that can help them cope more effectively.
- **Mindfulness and meditation**: These practices encourage individuals to focus on the present moment, helping to reduce anxiety and stress. Mindfulness allows people to observe their emotions without judgement, fostering better emotional regulation.
- **Creative outlets**: Engaging in activities like painting, writing, or playing music can help individuals express their feelings in a healthy way, providing an emotional release while also fostering a sense of accomplishment and enjoyment.

Unhealthy coping strategies, on the other hand, may provide temporary relief but ultimately contribute to more significant problems in the long run. These maladaptive methods often avoid or suppress emotions rather than addressing them directly. Examples of unhealthy coping strategies include:

- **Substance abuse**: Many individuals turn to alcohol or drugs to escape stress or emotional pain. While these substances may provide temporary relief, they can lead to dependency, health issues, and worsening emotional states.
- **Emotional eating**: Some people cope with stress by overeating, especially unhealthy foods, as a way to comfort themselves. While this might provide short-term satisfaction, it can lead to health problems such as obesity, diabetes, and further emotional distress.
- **Procrastination or avoidance**: Avoiding responsibilities or difficult situations can temporarily reduce anxiety, but it often leads to increased stress in the long term as tasks pile up or problems go unaddressed.

- **Aggression or lashing out**: Some individuals cope with stress by becoming angry or aggressive towards others. This behaviour damages relationships and does not resolve the underlying emotional issue, often leading to feelings of guilt or shame afterward.

Recognizing the difference between healthy and unhealthy coping mechanisms is crucial for promoting positive mental health. Individuals who rely on unhealthy strategies may find themselves stuck in negative behavioural cycles, whereas those who develop adaptive coping skills are better equipped to handle stress and challenges in constructive ways.

How Stress, Anxiety, and Trauma Influence Coping Styles

Stress, anxiety, and trauma are key factors that influence an individual's choice of coping strategies. These emotional states can disrupt normal cognitive processes, making it more difficult to regulate emotions and respond to challenges rationally. The coping mechanisms people adopt in response to stress often depend on the intensity of the stressor, their personality, past experiences, and emotional resilience.

Stress and Its Role in Shaping Coping Behaviour

Stress is a natural part of life, and how individuals respond to stress can vary widely. While some people are able to manage stress effectively through problem-solving and healthy outlets like exercise, others may feel overwhelmed and resort to avoidance or harmful behaviours. Chronic stress, in particular, can take a significant toll on both physical and mental health. If stress is not managed properly, it can lead to burnout, depression, or anxiety disorders.

Stress triggers the body's "fight or flight" response, activating the release of stress hormones like cortisol. This can lead to heightened emotions, difficulty concentrating, and irritability. In this state, individuals may become more impulsive and less likely to use healthy coping strategies. Over time, if stress becomes unmanageable, individuals may develop maladaptive behaviours like substance abuse, aggression, or social withdrawal as a way to cope.

Anxiety and the Development of Coping Mechanisms

Anxiety is closely related to stress but typically involves more prolonged worry or fear about future events. Individuals with anxiety may develop coping strategies centred around control or avoidance. For example, someone with social anxiety might cope by avoiding social situations altogether, while someone with generalised anxiety might engage in excessive planning or overthinking to try to prevent bad outcomes.

Anxiety often leads to over-reliance on avoidance as a coping mechanism. Avoidance may temporarily reduce anxiety by removing the immediate stressor, but it ultimately reinforces the anxiety by preventing the individual from facing and overcoming their fears. Over time, this can lead to more significant disruptions in life, such as avoiding work, social interactions, or even daily responsibilities.

The Lasting Impact of Trauma on Coping Styles

Traumatic experiences, particularly those that occur in childhood, can have a profound and lasting effect on an individual's coping mechanisms. Trauma disrupts the normal development of emotional regulation skills and may cause individuals to adopt coping strategies that are geared toward survival rather than long-term emotional health.

For example, individuals who have experienced trauma may develop hypervigilance, constantly scanning for potential threats and feeling on edge. This heightened state of alertness can make it difficult to relax, leading to coping mechanisms such as substance abuse or social isolation as an attempt to numb or escape from these feelings.

Trauma survivors may also struggle with emotional regulation, leading to difficulty managing intense emotions like anger, fear, or sadness. Without healthy coping mechanisms in place, they may resort to unhealthy behaviours like self-harm or aggression as a way to release pent-up emotions. Therapeutic interventions such as trauma-focused therapy are often necessary to help individuals develop healthier coping mechanisms and process their trauma in a constructive way.

The Importance of Emotional Regulation and Self-Awareness

Emotional regulation refers to the ability to manage and respond to emotions in a healthy and constructive manner. It is a critical component of effective coping and overall emotional well-being. Individuals with strong emotional regulation skills are better able to process stress and negative emotions without resorting to harmful coping mechanisms. On the other hand, poor emotional regulation can lead to impulsive behaviours and difficulty managing stress.

Self-awareness is closely tied to emotional regulation. It involves recognizing one's emotional state and understanding how emotions influence thoughts, behaviours, and decisions. When individuals are self-aware, they can identify when they are feeling overwhelmed or stressed and take steps to manage those emotions before they lead to negative behaviours.

For example, someone who is self-aware may notice that they tend to reach for junk food when stressed. By recognizing this pattern, they can make a conscious effort to replace that behaviour with a healthier alternative, such as going for a walk or practising deep breathing exercises. Self-awareness also helps individuals recognize the triggers that lead to unhealthy coping behaviours, allowing them to avoid or address those triggers proactively.

Techniques for Improving Emotional Regulation and Coping

Developing strong emotional regulation skills and healthy coping mechanisms requires practice and self-reflection. Some techniques that can help individuals improve their ability to cope with stress and manage emotions include:

1. **Mindfulness meditation**: Mindfulness helps individuals become more attuned to their emotions and thoughts without becoming overwhelmed by them. By practising mindfulness, individuals can develop greater emotional regulation and reduce impulsive reactions to stress.

2. **Cognitive restructuring**: This technique involves identifying and challenging negative thought patterns that contribute to stress and emotional distress. By replacing these thoughts with more balanced and realistic perspectives, individuals can reduce the intensity of negative emotions and develop healthier coping mechanisms.

3. **Physical activity**: Regular exercise is an effective way to reduce stress, improve

mood, and enhance emotional regulation. Physical activity releases endorphins, which are natural mood boosters, and provides a healthy outlet for managing negative emotions.

4. **Building a support system**: Having a network of supportive friends, family members, or a therapist can provide individuals with emotional support and guidance during stressful times. A strong support system helps individuals develop resilience and manage challenges more effectively.

5. **Stress management techniques**: Learning to manage stress through techniques such as deep breathing, progressive muscle relaxation, or time management can prevent stress from escalating and leading to unhealthy coping behaviours.

The Role of Habits in Shaping Daily Behavior

Habits play an essential role in our daily lives. They are behaviours we perform automatically, often without conscious thought, and they significantly influence our actions, decisions, and routines. Understanding how habits form, why they persist, and how they can be changed is crucial for personal growth and self-improvement. This chapter will examine the psychology of habits, the process of breaking unwanted habits, and the strategies needed to cultivate new, healthier patterns of behaviour.

How Habits Form and Influence Behavior

Habits are behaviours that have been repeated so often that they become ingrained in our daily routines. They develop through a process known as habit formation, which involves three key components: the cue, the routine, and the reward.

- **Cue**: The cue is the trigger that initiates the habit. It could be an external event, like the time of day or a specific location, or it could be an internal feeling, such as stress or hunger. Cues signal the brain that it's time to begin the habitual action.
- **Routine**: The routine is the behaviour itself, the action taken in response to the cue. This could be something as simple as brushing your teeth when you wake up or checking your phone every time you receive a notification.
- **Reward**: The reward is the positive outcome that reinforces the behaviour. It's

the satisfaction or relief you feel after completing the routine. For instance, the clean feeling after brushing your teeth or the sense of connection after responding to a message. Rewards create a sense of pleasure or fulfilment, which strengthens the habit over time.

Once this loop—cue, routine, and reward—becomes established, the behaviour begins to happen automatically. The brain learns to associate the cue with the routine and the reward, making the behaviour more likely to occur the next time the cue appears. As a result, habits can become deeply ingrained, influencing much of our daily behaviour without us even realising it.

While some habits are beneficial, such as exercising regularly or eating healthy meals, others can be detrimental to our health or productivity. Because habits operate largely on autopilot, they can be difficult to change, especially when the rewards are immediate, even if the long-term consequences are negative (e.g., smoking or overeating).

The Science Behind Breaking Bad Habits and Forming Good Ones

Breaking bad habits requires more than just willpower. It involves understanding how the habit works and finding ways to interrupt the automatic loop of cue, routine, and reward. Similarly, forming good habits involves creating new loops that reinforce positive behaviours. The science of habit formation and change offers valuable insights into how this process can be managed effectively.

The Challenge of Breaking Bad Habits

Bad habits are often challenging to break because they are ingrained in the brain's neural pathways. Every time a habit is performed, the connections between neurons in the brain strengthen, making the behaviour more automatic and harder to disrupt. To break a habit, it's not enough to simply stop the behaviour; the underlying cue and reward need to be addressed.

One effective method for breaking bad habits is to identify the **cue** that triggers the behaviour. By becoming more aware of the situations, emotions, or environmental factors that lead to the habit, it's possible to create a plan for avoiding or managing those cues. For example, if stress triggers overeating, finding alternative ways to manage stress, such as exercising or practising relaxation techniques, can help reduce the likelihood of turning to food for comfort.

Another important step in breaking bad habits is to replace the **routine**. Instead of trying to eliminate the habit entirely, it's often more effective to substitute a healthier behaviour in its place. For example, someone who wants to quit smoking might replace the act of smoking with chewing gum or going for a short walk. The new routine should still provide some form of reward to maintain motivation and reinforce the new behaviour.

Lastly, it's crucial to focus on **reward**. The brain is wired to seek out rewards, and breaking a habit becomes much easier if the new behaviour is also satisfying in some way. For example, if a person is trying to quit eating junk food, they can focus on the long-term reward of feeling healthier and having more energy, rather than the short-term pleasure of eating sugary snacks.

Forming Good Habits

Just as breaking a habit requires disrupting the cue-routine-reward loop, forming new, positive habits involves building a new loop that supports the desired behaviour. The process of habit formation relies on consistency and repetition. The more often a behaviour is repeated in response to a cue, the more automatic it becomes over time.

One of the most effective strategies for forming good habits is **starting small**. Instead of trying to implement drastic changes all at once, it's often more successful to begin with small, manageable behaviours. For example, someone who wants to develop a habit of exercising regularly could start with just 10 minutes of activity each day, gradually increasing the duration as the habit becomes more ingrained. Starting small makes the new behaviour less overwhelming and increases the likelihood of success.

Another helpful strategy is **pairing a new habit with an existing one**, a technique known as "habit stacking." For example, if someone already has a well-established morning routine, such as making coffee, they can add a new habit—like drinking a glass of water or stretching—immediately after making coffee. The established habit acts as a cue for the new behaviour, making it easier to remember and repeat.

Strategies for Behavioral Change and Personal Growth

Changing behaviour, whether it's breaking a bad habit or forming a new one, requires a combination of awareness, planning, and consistency. Here are some key strategies for successfully changing habits and fostering personal growth:

1. **Self-Awareness and Reflection**: The first step in any behaviour change is becoming aware of current habits and the factors that contribute to them. Reflecting on why certain habits exist, when they occur, and how they make you feel can provide valuable insight into the changes that need to be made. Keeping a habit journal or using a habit-tracking app can help increase self-awareness and identify patterns in behaviour.

2. **Setting Clear Goals**: Having a specific goal is essential for creating new habits or breaking old ones. Vague goals like "I want to be healthier" are harder to achieve than specific goals like "I want to exercise for 30 minutes three times a week." Clear, measurable goals provide a target to work toward and help track progress.

3. **Building an Environment for Success**: The environment plays a significant role in shaping habits. By modifying your surroundings to support new habits and reduce the influence of old ones, you can increase the chances of success. For example, if you're trying to eat healthier, keeping nutritious snacks easily accessible and removing junk food from your home can help reinforce your new habit.

4. **Accountability and Support**: Having someone to hold you accountable, whether it's a friend, family member, or coach, can be a powerful motivator for behaviour change. Sharing your goals with someone else creates a sense of responsibility and encourages follow-through. Supportive environments also foster personal growth by providing encouragement and feedback along the way.

5. **Rewarding Progress**: Celebrating small wins is essential for maintaining motivation during the habit-change process. Recognizing progress, no matter

how small, provides positive reinforcement that helps solidify new habits. Whether it's treating yourself to something enjoyable or simply acknowledging your accomplishments, rewards help make the process of habit formation more enjoyable.

6. **Consistency and Patience**: Building new habits takes time and requires consistent effort. The more a behaviour is repeated, the more automatic it becomes, but this doesn't happen overnight. Research suggests that it can take anywhere from a few weeks to several months to establish a new habit, depending on the complexity of the behaviour and individual differences. Patience is key to sustaining long-term behavioural change.

The Impact of Motivation and Goals on Behavior

Motivation is a key driving force behind human behaviour, influencing how people act, what they prioritise, and how they make decisions. It shapes the way individuals approach tasks and challenges, and it is a central factor in goal-setting and achievement.

The Difference Between Intrinsic and Extrinsic Motivation

Motivation can be categorised into two main types: intrinsic and extrinsic. Understanding the differences between these forms of motivation can shed light on why people behave the way they do and how they can better harness their motivation to achieve their goals.

Intrinsic Motivation

Intrinsic motivation refers to the internal drive to engage in an activity for its own sake, rather than for any external reward or recognition. People who are intrinsically motivated find enjoyment or personal satisfaction in the task itself. This type of motivation often leads to a deeper sense of engagement and fulfilment because the individual is driven by a genuine interest or passion.

For example, a person who enjoys painting might do so simply because they find it relaxing or creatively stimulating, regardless of whether anyone else sees their work. Similarly, someone who loves learning might pursue education not for grades or accolades, but because they find the acquisition of knowledge personally rewarding.

Studies have shown that intrinsic motivation is often more sustainable and leads to higher levels of satisfaction and performance over time. When people are intrinsically motivated, they tend to stick with tasks longer, take greater pride in their work, and experience a greater sense of well-being.

Extrinsic Motivation

Extrinsic motivation, on the other hand, is driven by external factors, such as rewards, recognition, or the avoidance of negative consequences. When someone is extrinsically motivated, their behaviour is influenced by the desire to gain something outside of the activity itself—whether it's money, praise, or approval.

An example of extrinsic motivation would be an employee working hard on a project primarily to receive a bonus or a student studying to earn high grades rather than for the joy of learning. While extrinsic rewards can be powerful motivators, they may not always lead to lasting satisfaction. Once the external reward is removed, the motivation to continue the behaviour often fades.

However, extrinsic motivation is not inherently negative. In many cases, it can be highly effective, especially when paired with intrinsic motivation. For example, an athlete might train hard both because they love their sport (intrinsic motivation) and because they want to win a competition (extrinsic motivation). The key is finding the right balance between intrinsic and extrinsic motivators, as both can play important roles in driving behaviour.

How Setting Goals Influences Daily Actions

Goal-setting is a powerful tool that directs behaviour and gives people a clear sense of purpose. Goals provide a framework for action, helping individuals prioritise their efforts and stay focused on what matters most. Whether the goals are short-term, like completing a project by the end of the week, or long-term, such as pursuing a career path, they guide day-to-day decisions and behaviour.

The Power of Specific Goals

One of the most important factors in effective goal-setting is specificity. Research has shown that people are more likely to achieve their goals when they are clear and well-defined. Vague goals, like "I want to be healthier," are harder to achieve because they lack direction. In contrast, specific goals, such as "I want to exercise for 30 minutes five times a week," provide a clear target to work toward.

When individuals set specific goals, they can break them down into actionable steps. This clarity allows them to focus on the immediate tasks needed to move closer to their objectives. For example, someone aiming to complete a marathon might create a detailed training plan, scheduling regular runs, rest days, and gradual increases in distance.

Goal-Setting and Motivation

Goals play a crucial role in maintaining motivation. When people set goals that are personally meaningful, they are more likely to stay motivated and committed to achieving them. This connection between goals and motivation is closely tied to both intrinsic and extrinsic motivators. For example, an intrinsically motivated person might set a goal to improve their skills in a hobby they love, while an extrinsically motivated person might aim to achieve a promotion at work to gain recognition and financial rewards.

Goals also provide a sense of progress and accomplishment, which reinforces motivation. Each small success along the way, such as reaching a milestone or completing a step, gives a sense of achievement that fuels the drive to continue. Without clear goals, people may feel aimless or lose motivation, as they have no clear direction or way to measure progress.

The Role of Deadlines and Accountability

Deadlines and accountability are additional factors that enhance the effectiveness of goal-setting. When people set specific deadlines for their goals, they create a sense of urgency that encourages action. Deadlines help to prevent procrastination and push individuals to focus on completing tasks within a certain timeframe.

Accountability is also important in goal-setting. Sharing goals with others or seeking feedback can create external pressure to follow through on commitments. For instance, someone who commits to a fitness goal by joining a group exercise class or working with a personal trainer may be more likely to stick with their routine because they feel accountable to others.

The Importance of Aligning Behavior with Long-Term Aspirations

While setting short-term goals is important, it's equally crucial to ensure that daily behaviour aligns with long-term aspirations. Many people have big dreams or long-term visions for their lives, but they struggle to bridge the gap between their daily actions and their future goals. Aligning behaviour with long-term aspirations requires ongoing reflection, discipline, and intentionality.

Consistency Over Time

Consistency is a key factor in turning long-term aspirations into reality. Small, consistent actions taken over time can lead to significant progress, even if the immediate results are not always visible. This is why it's essential to break down long-term goals into manageable steps and integrate them into daily routines.

For example, someone with a long-term aspiration to write a book might commit to writing 500 words every day. While the daily effort may seem small, the cumulative result over months or years could be the completion of a full manuscript. Aligning daily behaviour with long-term aspirations requires patience and persistence, as progress may not always be immediately apparent.

Avoiding Short-Term Distractions

One of the biggest challenges in aligning behaviour with long-term goals is avoiding the temptation of short-term distractions. In today's fast-paced world, it's easy to get sidetracked by immediate rewards or fleeting pleasures that don't contribute to long-term success. For example, spending hours scrolling through social media may provide short-term entertainment, but it often pulls people away from meaningful work or personal growth.

To stay aligned with long-term aspirations, it's important to prioritise activities that contribute to those goals and minimise distractions that don't. This requires self-discipline and a strong sense of purpose. By regularly reflecting on their long-term vision, individuals can stay focused on what truly matters, even when short-term distractions arise.

Self-Reflection and Adaptation

Aligning behaviour with long-term aspirations also involves regular self-reflection. People's goals and priorities can evolve over time, and it's important to periodically assess whether current actions are still aligned with future desires. Self-reflection allows individuals to make adjustments, refine their goals, and ensure that their behaviour continues to support their evolving aspirations.

In some cases, this may involve letting go of old habits or goals that no longer serve a purpose. For example, someone who initially pursued a certain career path might realise after several years that their interests have changed. Self-reflection enables them to shift their focus and realign their behaviour with new, more meaningful goals.

The Power of Choice: Taking Responsibility for Your Actions

Choice is one of the most defining aspects of human behaviour. Every decision, no matter how small, carries with it a consequence that shapes our lives in profound ways. Understanding how choice operates, the role of personal responsibility, and the debate between free will and determinism, can greatly influence the way we approach our daily behaviour. This chapter will examine how personal responsibility shapes actions, explore philosophical debates about free will and determinism, and discuss why recognizing and owning our choices is crucial for fostering behavioural change.

How Personal Responsibility Shapes Behavior

Personal responsibility refers to the accountability individuals take for their actions and decisions. It is the recognition that, despite external factors, we are ultimately in control of how we respond to situations. Accepting personal responsibility is vital for developing a sense of agency and empowerment, as it encourages individuals to actively shape their lives instead of passively reacting to circumstances.

Accountability in Decision-Making

When people take responsibility for their actions, they are more likely to engage in thoughtful decision-making. Being accountable means understanding that every action has consequences, both positive and negative. For example, if someone makes a poor financial decision, accepting responsibility for it encourages them to learn from the mistake, correct the behaviour, and make better choices in the future. In contrast, those who deflect responsibility might blame external factors, leading to repeated mistakes without meaningful personal growth.

Personal responsibility also fosters a sense of ownership over outcomes. When individuals take responsibility for their actions, they can reflect on what they can control and what they cannot. By focusing on what they can influence, they become more proactive and resilient in the face of challenges. This sense of accountability is foundational for self-improvement because it emphasises the role of individual agency in shaping one's circumstances.

The Role of External Influences

While personal responsibility is important, it is also essential to recognize the role of external influences, such as social, economic, and environmental factors. These factors can affect the choices available to individuals, but they do not absolve people of their responsibility for how they respond to these circumstances. For instance, while someone may grow up in a disadvantaged community with fewer opportunities, they still have choices regarding how they engage with the challenges they face.

By acknowledging external influences while maintaining personal responsibility, individuals strike a balance between understanding the factors that shape their lives and taking ownership of their actions within those constraints. This balance allows people to navigate life's complexities while still maintaining a sense of control and responsibility for their behaviour.

The Concept of Free Will and Determinism in Human Behavior

The philosophical debate between free will and determinism is central to understanding human behaviour. It raises fundamental questions about whether individuals truly have control over their choices or whether their actions are predetermined by external forces, genetics, or other factors beyond their control.

Free Will: The Power to Choose

Free will is the idea that individuals have the ability to make choices independent of external pressures. According to this perspective, humans possess the autonomy to decide their actions, making them morally and ethically accountable for their behaviour. Free will implies that people are not merely products of their environment or biology, but rather, they have the capacity to reflect on their circumstances and make intentional decisions.

Those who believe in free will argue that it is this very capacity for choice that gives life meaning. Without free will, the concept of responsibility would lose its relevance, as people would not be accountable for actions that were predetermined. Free will is often linked to the sense of personal empowerment—when people believe they can choose their path, they are more likely to take ownership of their behaviour and make conscious efforts to change or improve.

Determinism: The Influence of External Forces

On the other hand, determinism posits that human behaviour is shaped by external and internal forces that are beyond an individual's control. According to determinists, everything from genetics to upbringing and societal influences plays a role in dictating how people behave. In this view, choice is an illusion, as every decision is the result of prior causes, not free will.

For example, a determinist might argue that a person's career path is influenced by the education system they were born into, their socioeconomic status, and the values instilled in them during childhood. In this framework, individuals are seen as products of their environment, acting based on predetermined factors rather than making truly independent choices.

Determinism challenges the idea of personal responsibility by suggesting that, if actions are dictated by external forces, holding people accountable for their behaviour may be unfair. However, even in a deterministic framework, individuals still experience the illusion of choice, which means they can still operate within certain boundaries to make changes in their lives.

The Interplay Between Free Will and Determinism

Many contemporary perspectives on human behaviour suggest that the debate between free will and determinism is not an either/or proposition but a spectrum. While it is undeniable that factors like biology, environment, and social conditions shape behaviour, there remains a space for individual choice and responsibility. People may be influenced by their circumstances, but they also possess the ability to reflect on those influences and make intentional decisions within those constraints.

Recognizing this interplay allows for a more nuanced understanding of human behaviour. It acknowledges that while individuals are shaped by external forces, they still possess the capacity for self-awareness and change. This understanding reinforces the importance of taking responsibility for one's actions, even in the face of external challenges.

Why Understanding Your Choices Is Key to Behavioral Change

The ability to recognize and understand one's choices is fundamental to making meaningful behavioural changes. When people are aware of the decisions they make, they gain insight into the patterns of their behaviour, enabling them to take deliberate steps toward change.

Awareness of Habitual Choices

Many behaviours are driven by habitual choices, which often go unnoticed because they are automatic. For example, a person might unconsciously eat unhealthy snacks every evening while watching television. Over time, this habit becomes ingrained, influencing their health and well-being. Without conscious awareness of this pattern, it can be difficult to make changes.

Becoming aware of these automatic choices is the first step toward change. Once individuals recognize the habits that shape their behaviour, they can take active steps to replace unhealthy habits with healthier ones. This process of self-awareness is essential for anyone seeking to improve their life, as it empowers individuals to take control of their choices rather than being controlled by them.

The Power of Intentional Decision-Making

Intentional decision-making is the practice of consciously evaluating one's choices and their potential consequences. It involves pausing to reflect on the motivations, desires, and outcomes associated with a particular decision before taking action. By practising intentional decision-making, people can align their behaviour with their values and long-term goals.

For example, someone who is trying to improve their financial situation might practise intentional decision-making by considering the long-term impact of their spending habits. Rather than impulsively buying something, they pause to reflect on whether the purchase aligns with their goal of saving money. Over time, this practice of intentional decision-making can lead to more disciplined behaviour and greater control over one's life.

Responsibility in Behavioral Change

Taking responsibility for one's choices is a powerful catalyst for behavioural change. When people accept that they are in control of their actions, they are more likely to take proactive steps to improve themselves. Conversely, those who deflect responsibility or blame external factors are less likely to engage in meaningful self-reflection or take action toward change.

Accepting responsibility also involves acknowledging the consequences of past choices, both positive and negative. This self-awareness can be uncomfortable, but it is an essential part of personal growth. By owning past mistakes, individuals can learn valuable lessons that inform future decisions. At the same time, taking responsibility for positive actions reinforces the sense of agency and empowers people to continue making choices that align with their goals.

Behavioural Change: Strategies for Lasting Transformation

Changing behaviour, especially long-standing habits, can feel overwhelming. However, with the right strategies, the process becomes manageable and achievable. This chapter explores practical approaches to understanding and transforming behaviour, highlights the effectiveness of cognitive-behavioural therapy (CBT), and emphasises the role of mindfulness and self-reflection in creating sustainable change.

Practical Approaches to Understanding and Changing Behaviour

To successfully change behaviour, it is essential to first understand the motivations, triggers, and patterns that sustain current actions. Behavioural change doesn't happen in isolation; it often requires examining thoughts, emotions, and environmental factors that influence behaviour. Below are several key approaches that provide a foundation for understanding and implementing behavioural changes.

Recognizing Triggers and Patterns

One of the first steps in changing behaviour is identifying the triggers that lead to certain actions. Triggers are specific situations, emotions, or thoughts that prompt particular behaviours. For example, stress at work may trigger unhealthy eating habits, or boredom may lead to excessive social media use. Identifying these triggers helps individuals recognize patterns in their behaviour, which is crucial for making changes.

Once triggers are identified, the next step is recognizing the patterns they create. Behaviour often follows a predictable sequence: a trigger leads to an action, and the action results in a consequence, either positive or negative. By examining these sequences, individuals can pinpoint where change is needed and develop strategies to alter their responses.

Setting Clear, Achievable Goals

Change becomes more attainable when broken down into clear, specific, and measurable goals. Vague intentions, such as "I want to be healthier," often lack the structure needed to sustain progress. Instead, setting clear goals, such as "I will go for a 30-minute walk every morning," creates a concrete plan for action. Goals should be realistic and achievable to avoid frustration and loss of motivation. Starting small allows individuals to build momentum and gradually increase the difficulty of their goals over time.

Monitoring Progress and Adjusting as Needed

Behavioural change is rarely a linear process. It's essential to monitor progress regularly to assess whether the strategies employed are working effectively. Keeping a journal or using apps that track behaviour can provide insight into areas of improvement and where adjustments are necessary. Reflecting on progress also fosters self-awareness, helping individuals recognize when they are falling back into old patterns. If obstacles arise, adapting strategies and trying new approaches can help maintain momentum toward lasting change.

Cognitive-Behavioral Therapy (CBT) for Personal Growth

Cognitive-behavioural therapy (CBT) is a widely used approach that focuses on changing patterns of thinking and behaviour. Originally developed for treating mental health issues, CBT's principles can also be applied to general behavioural change. It is based on the idea that thoughts, emotions, and behaviours are interconnected, and changing one aspect can lead to positive changes in the others.

Challenging Negative Thought Patterns

CBT emphasises the importance of identifying and challenging negative or unhelpful thought patterns that contribute to unwanted behaviour. For example, someone trying to quit smoking may have the belief, "I'm too stressed to quit right now." These automatic thoughts often reinforce behaviours that individuals want to change. By recognizing these thoughts, individuals can challenge their validity and replace them with more constructive alternatives, such as, "Quitting smoking will reduce my stress in the long run."

Challenging and replacing negative thought patterns leads to changes in emotional responses and behaviour. As people learn to think more positively or realistically about their situation, they are less likely to engage in self-defeating behaviours and more likely to adopt healthier habits.

Behavioural Activation

Another key element of CBT is behavioural activation, which involves increasing engagement in positive activities to counteract feelings of sadness or anxiety. Often, individuals avoid tasks or situations that they associate with discomfort or stress, leading to patterns of procrastination or inactivity. Behavioural activation encourages individuals to gradually face and engage in these activities, which in turn leads to improved mood and reduced avoidance behaviours.

For example, someone experiencing social anxiety might avoid attending social events due to fear of embarrassment. Behavioural activation would encourage them to gradually expose themselves to social situations, starting with smaller gatherings before working up to larger events. This process not only improves confidence but also reduces the avoidance behaviour that maintains anxiety.

Developing Coping Skills

CBT also focuses on developing healthy coping skills to replace maladaptive behaviours. For instance, if stress triggers overeating, an individual can learn alternative ways to cope with stress, such as relaxation techniques or physical exercise. By consistently practising these new coping mechanisms, individuals can weaken the connection between stress and overeating, leading to lasting behavioural change.

The Role of Mindfulness and Self-Reflection in Behavioral Change

Mindfulness and self-reflection are powerful tools for creating lasting change because they help individuals stay present, recognize automatic behaviours, and reflect on their intentions. These practices foster greater self-awareness, allowing individuals to respond thoughtfully rather than react impulsively.

Mindfulness and Present-Moment Awareness

Mindfulness involves paying attention to the present moment without judgement. It helps individuals become aware of their thoughts, emotions, and behaviours as they occur, rather than operating on autopilot. By practising mindfulness, individuals can interrupt automatic responses that lead to unwanted behaviour.

For example, someone trying to change their eating habits might practise mindful eating, which involves paying close attention to the taste, texture, and experience of eating. This approach reduces the likelihood of mindless snacking or overeating, as the individual becomes more aware of the signals of hunger and fullness.

Mindfulness can also be applied to emotional regulation. Instead of reacting impulsively to stress or frustration, mindfulness encourages individuals to pause and observe their emotions without judgement. This allows them to respond more calmly and constructively to challenging situations.

Self-Reflection for Personal Growth

Self-reflection is the practice of regularly evaluating one's actions, thoughts, and emotions. It plays a key role in behavioural change because it encourages individuals to assess their progress, recognize setbacks, and make adjustments. Self-reflection can be done through journaling, meditation, or simply taking time at the end of each day to think about what went well and what could be improved.

Regular self-reflection fosters accountability and helps individuals stay aligned with their goals. By reflecting on both successes and failures, individuals can learn from their experiences and continuously refine their approach to change.

Combining Mindfulness and CBT Techniques

Mindfulness can complement CBT techniques by helping individuals remain aware of their thoughts and behaviours as they work to change them. While CBT focuses on challenging and restructuring negative thoughts, mindfulness helps individuals recognize those thoughts in real time, allowing them to apply CBT strategies more effectively. Together, these approaches create a comprehensive framework for behavioural change that addresses both conscious and subconscious patterns.

Strategies for Lasting Behavioural Change

Lasting transformation requires a combination of strategies that address both immediate behaviours and the underlying patterns that sustain them. Below are several key strategies that promote enduring behavioural change.

Start with Small, Consistent Steps

One of the most effective ways to create lasting change is by starting with small, manageable steps. Trying to overhaul behaviour all at once can lead to frustration and burnout. Instead, focus on making incremental changes that build over time. For example, if the goal is to exercise regularly, starting with a 10-minute walk each day is more sustainable than attempting an hour-long workout right away. Gradually increasing the intensity and duration allows the new behaviour to become a natural part of daily life.

Develop a Support System

Having a support system can significantly enhance the likelihood of success. Whether it's friends, family, or a coach, sharing goals with others creates accountability and provides encouragement during difficult moments. A support system can offer feedback, celebrate successes, and help navigate setbacks, making the process of change more manageable.

Replace Negative Habits with Positive Ones

Behavioural change often involves not just eliminating negative habits but replacing them with positive alternatives. For instance, if someone wants to reduce their screen time before bed, they might replace that habit with reading a book or practising relaxation exercises. Replacing an unwanted behaviour with a healthier alternative makes it easier to break the habit cycle and sustain the change over time.

Be Patient and Persistent

Changing behaviour is a gradual process that requires patience and persistence. It's common to experience setbacks or slip back into old habits from time to time. The key is to stay committed to the process and view setbacks as learning opportunities rather than failures. Over time, with consistent effort, new behaviours become ingrained, and lasting change is achieved.

Overcoming Behavioral Challenges

Many individuals face behavioural challenges that hinder personal growth and well-being. Whether it's procrastination, addiction, or other negative patterns, these behaviours can often feel overwhelming, leading to frustration and self-doubt. However, by understanding these behaviours and employing effective strategies, individuals can overcome these challenges and foster positive change.

Addressing Procrastination, Addiction, and Other Negative Patterns

Procrastination: Understanding and Overcoming Delays in Action

Procrastination is the habitual delay of tasks despite knowing there will be negative consequences. It's one of the most common challenges people face when trying to change behaviour. While procrastination may seem like a time management issue, it often stems from deeper emotional or psychological factors, such as fear of failure, perfectionism, or feeling overwhelmed by the magnitude of a task.

To overcome procrastination, it's crucial to identify its root causes. For many, procrastination provides temporary relief from anxiety or discomfort associated with a task. However, this avoidance ultimately leads to greater stress and guilt. Below are practical steps to combat procrastination:

1. **Break tasks into smaller, manageable steps**: Large tasks can seem daunting, which often leads to avoidance. Breaking them into smaller, more achievable parts

makes it easier to get started and reduces the feeling of being overwhelmed.

2. **Set deadlines and prioritise tasks**: Establishing clear deadlines and prioritising the most important tasks helps prevent the habit of putting things off indefinitely. It also creates a sense of urgency that can motivate action.

3. **Reward progress**: Creating a reward system can reinforce positive behaviour. After completing a task, even if it's small, rewarding yourself can help build momentum and increase motivation.

4. **Develop self-compassion**: Procrastinators often struggle with self-criticism, which can reinforce avoidance. Learning to be compassionate with oneself during setbacks reduces anxiety and encourages a healthier approach to tackling tasks.

Addiction: Breaking Free from Destructive Cycles

Addiction, whether to substances, behaviours, or even digital media, is another significant behavioural challenge. Addiction is often characterised by an inability to stop engaging in certain behaviours despite knowing their negative consequences. It impacts emotional well-being, relationships, and overall quality of life.

To address addiction, individuals need to understand that it's not simply a matter of willpower. Addiction alters brain chemistry, creating intense cravings and reinforcing unhealthy patterns. Effective strategies for overcoming addiction include:

1. **Acknowledge the problem**: Recognizing that addiction is affecting one's life is the first step toward recovery. Without acknowledgement, it's difficult to develop a plan for change.
2. **Seek professional support**: Addiction is complex and often requires professional intervention. Therapy, counselling, or support groups like Alcoholics Anonymous (AA) or Narcotics Anonymous (NA) provide essential tools

and community support for overcoming addiction. Professional guidance can offer a structured approach to recovery, including addressing underlying emotional and psychological issues.

3. **Replace harmful behaviours with positive ones**: Substituting addictive behaviours with healthier alternatives is crucial for recovery. For example, engaging in physical activity, pursuing creative hobbies, or practising mindfulness can help redirect attention away from cravings.

4. **Build a support system**: Isolation can fuel addiction, while social support strengthens recovery. Surrounding oneself with supportive friends, family members, or groups who understand the challenges of addiction helps create accountability and encouragement.

Other Negative Patterns

Other behavioural patterns such as chronic stress, negative self-talk, and poor emotional regulation also hinder personal growth. These patterns are often reinforced over time and become automatic responses to various life circumstances. Addressing these challenges requires individuals to actively identify their triggers and implement strategies to break the cycle.

For example, chronic stress often results in unhealthy coping mechanisms such as overeating or lashing out at others. Recognizing these patterns and learning healthier coping techniques, such as practising relaxation exercises or seeking professional guidance, can prevent these behaviours from becoming ingrained. Similarly, replacing negative self-talk with affirmations and realistic assessments can reduce anxiety and encourage healthier thinking.

Recognizing Self-Sabotaging Behaviour

Self-sabotage refers to actions or thought patterns that prevent individuals from achieving their goals. This behaviour often stems from fear of failure, fear of success, or deeply ingrained limiting beliefs. Self-sabotaging behaviour can manifest in various ways, including procrastination, avoidance, or engaging in destructive habits.

Identifying Self-Sabotaging Patterns

Recognizing self-sabotage requires honest self-reflection. It's important to examine patterns of behaviour that continually undermine progress, especially when goals are within reach. Common signs of self-sabotage include:

1. **Avoiding tasks or goals**: Consistently putting off work that could lead to success is a hallmark of self-sabotage. For example, delaying studying for an important exam despite knowing the consequences.
2. **Engaging in negative self-talk**: Thoughts like "I'm not good enough" or "I'll never succeed" reinforce feelings of inadequacy and prevent individuals from taking steps toward their goals.

3. **Creating unnecessary conflicts**: Sometimes individuals unconsciously create conflict in personal or professional relationships to divert attention away from their own shortcomings.
4. **Setting unrealistic expectations**: Setting goals that are too ambitious can lead to burnout or feelings of failure, causing individuals to give up altogether.

Overcoming Self-Sabotage

Breaking free from self-sabotaging behaviour requires conscious effort and self-awareness. Here are strategies to address and overcome these behaviours:

1. **Challenge limiting beliefs**: Many self-sabotaging behaviours are rooted in limiting beliefs that are not based on reality. It's essential to question these beliefs and replace them with more empowering ones. For instance, instead of thinking, "I always fail," consider "I've

succeeded in the past, and I can do it again."

2. **Set realistic goals**: While ambition is important, setting achievable and realistic goals is essential for avoiding self-sabotage. Realistic goals provide a sense of progress and prevent feelings of overwhelm or failure.

3. **Develop self-compassion**: Treating oneself with kindness, especially after setbacks, reduces the tendency to engage in self-sabotaging behaviour. Rather than criticising oneself for mistakes, adopting a mindset of learning and growth fosters resilience.

4. **Seek accountability**: Sharing goals with a trusted friend, mentor, or coach creates external accountability and reduces the likelihood of engaging in self-sabotaging behaviour.

Building Resilience and Fostering Positive Change

Resilience, the ability to bounce back from setbacks and adapt to change, is a critical factor in overcoming behavioural challenges. Developing resilience not only helps individuals recover from failures but also strengthens their ability to pursue and maintain positive change.

Cultivating Resilience

Resilience is not an innate trait but a skill that can be developed through practice and intentional action. Building resilience requires adopting a mindset that embraces challenges as opportunities for growth rather than threats to success. Strategies for building resilience include:

1. **Develop a growth mindset**: Embracing a growth mindset means believing that abilities and behaviours can improve over time with effort and learning. Instead of seeing failure as an endpoint, individuals with a growth mindset view setbacks as opportunities to learn and improve.

2. **Practice self-care**: Physical and emotional well-being are foundational to resilience. Regular exercise, sufficient sleep, and healthy nutrition contribute to overall resilience, helping individuals handle stress and setbacks more effectively.

3. **Build strong relationships**: Resilient individuals often have a network of supportive relationships. Building and nurturing connections with family, friends, or colleagues provides emotional support during challenging times and reinforces positive behaviours.

4. **Develop problem-solving skills**: Resilience is closely linked to an individual's ability to solve problems effectively. By learning to approach challenges with a problem-solving mindset, individuals can reduce feelings of helplessness and take constructive action when facing obstacles.

Fostering Positive Change

Positive change is the ultimate goal of overcoming behavioural challenges. Building resilience and addressing procrastination, addiction, or self-sabotage are essential steps in creating lasting transformation. To foster positive change, individuals must maintain focus, patience, and consistency in their efforts. Below are key strategies for fostering positive change:

1. **Celebrate progress**: Recognizing and celebrating small victories along the way reinforces positive behaviour and builds momentum. Celebrating progress prevents discouragement and reminds individuals of the progress they've made.

2. **Create supportive environments**: Changing behaviour is easier in environments that support positive habits. This may involve removing triggers for negative behaviour or surrounding oneself with people who encourage and reinforce positive actions.

3. **Stay adaptable**: Flexibility is important when striving for change. Sometimes plans don't go as expected, and individuals may need to adjust their strategies. Staying adaptable allows individuals to learn from setbacks and continue moving forward.

The Impact of Relationships on Your Behaviour

Relationships play a crucial role in shaping human behaviour. From intimate partnerships to friendships and social connections, the relationships we form influence our thoughts, emotions, and actions. Whether positive or negative, these interactions contribute significantly to the way we respond to the world around us. Understanding how relationships affect behaviour is essential for personal growth, improving communication, resolving conflicts, and fostering healthier connections with others.

How Intimate and Social Relationships Affect Your Actions

Human behaviour is often a reflection of the relationships we cultivate. The influence of intimate relationships, such as those with a partner or close family members, tends to be more direct and profound, while social relationships, like friendships or community interactions, exert more subtle but equally important effects.

Intimate Relationships and Behavior

Intimate relationships, particularly romantic partnerships, have a strong impact on behaviour due to their emotional depth and closeness. In these relationships, individuals often act based on the needs, expectations, and emotions of their partner. For example, one might change certain habits, preferences, or behaviours to accommodate their partner's desires or to maintain harmony in the relationship. This can be both positive and negative depending on the dynamics of the relationship.

Positive intimate relationships encourage supportive behaviours, such as empathy, cooperation, and compromise. Partners in healthy relationships are more likely to engage in behaviours that foster mutual respect and understanding. On the other hand, negative intimate relationships can lead to stress, anxiety, and behaviours driven by insecurity or conflict. In some cases, individuals in unhealthy relationships may exhibit self-destructive behaviours or adopt coping mechanisms like avoidance or emotional withdrawal.

A significant aspect of intimate relationships is the emotional influence each partner has on the other. Emotional contagion—the phenomenon where one person's emotions influence another's—plays a major role in how partners react to situations. When one partner is upset, the other may adopt similar feelings, which can either lead to constructive problem-solving or escalate into conflict, depending on how emotions are managed.

Social Relationships and Behavior

While intimate relationships often exert a more immediate influence on behaviour, social relationships such as friendships, professional interactions, or community affiliations contribute to long-term behavioural patterns. The behaviour of individuals within a social circle can significantly affect decisions, attitudes, and habits. For instance, peer pressure in social groups can shape behaviour, especially when it comes to lifestyle choices, such as diet, exercise, and recreational activities.

Social groups also provide a sense of identity and belonging. People often adapt their behaviour to fit in with the values and norms of the group. This can lead to positive behaviours, such as engaging in group activities that promote well-being and personal growth. Conversely, it can also lead to negative behaviours if the group endorses unhealthy habits or toxic patterns.

The social comparison theory, which suggests that individuals evaluate themselves based on how they compare to others, also plays a role in shaping behaviour. In social settings, individuals may modify their behaviour to either match or differentiate themselves from their peers, depending on their desire for acceptance or distinction.

The Role of Communication and Conflict in Shaping Behaviour

Effective communication is the foundation of all relationships. The way individuals communicate—both verbally and nonverbally—greatly impacts their interactions and the behaviours that result from those interactions. In both intimate and social relationships, communication serves as a tool for expressing emotions, needs, and desires. When communication is clear, respectful, and empathetic, it fosters positive behaviours, strengthens relationships, and reduces the likelihood of conflict.

The Impact of Communication on Behavior

Positive communication involves active listening, empathy, and the ability to express oneself clearly without resorting to aggression or passive-aggressiveness. Individuals who communicate effectively are more likely to build trust, resolve disagreements, and maintain healthy relationships. This, in turn, encourages behaviours that promote connection and understanding, such as offering support, showing kindness, and being considerate of others' needs.

On the other hand, poor communication can lead to misunderstandings, frustration, and conflict. When communication breaks down, individuals may engage in negative behaviours, such as arguing, withdrawing, or avoiding confrontation altogether. Over time, these behaviours can erode the relationship, leading to further conflicts and unhealthy patterns.

Nonverbal communication—body language, tone of voice, facial expressions—also plays a critical role in shaping behaviour within relationships. Misinterpreting nonverbal cues can lead to confusion or assumptions that trigger defensive or unhelpful behaviours. For example, a person may perceive a partner's silence as disinterest or anger, leading to feelings of rejection or resentment, even if the silence was simply a reflection of thoughtfulness.

The Role of Conflict in Behavioral Change

Conflict is inevitable in relationships, but how it is handled significantly impacts the behaviour of those involved. Healthy conflict resolution allows individuals to address differences in a constructive manner, leading to personal growth and stronger relationships. When conflicts are resolved through open communication, compromise, and mutual understanding, both parties can learn from the experience, leading to positive changes in behaviour.

Conversely, unresolved conflict can have a detrimental effect on behaviour. If conflicts are left unaddressed or poorly managed, they can lead to lingering resentment, avoidance, or passive-aggressive actions. These behaviours not only strain the relationship but can also affect the individuals' overall well-being, leading to stress, anxiety, and emotional withdrawal.

To foster healthy relationships and encourage positive behavioural changes, it is essential to develop skills for managing conflict effectively. This includes maintaining calm during disagreements, listening to the other person's perspective, and working collaboratively to find solutions that satisfy both parties.

Building Healthier Relationships Through Self-Awareness

Self-awareness—the ability to recognize and understand one's emotions, thoughts, and behaviours—is a key factor in building and maintaining healthy relationships. Individuals who are self-aware are better equipped to manage their reactions, communicate effectively, and foster positive connections with others. By cultivating self-awareness, individuals can identify patterns of behaviour that may be detrimental to their relationships and take steps to change them.

The Role of Self-Awareness in Relationships

Self-awareness helps individuals recognize how their behaviour impacts others. For example, a person who is aware of their tendency to become defensive during arguments can consciously work to remain open and receptive when disagreements arise. Similarly, someone who is aware of their need for validation can communicate that need to their partner rather than expecting them to guess or feel frustrated when it isn't met.

By practising self-awareness, individuals can also identify triggers that lead to negative behaviours, such as becoming easily irritated or withdrawing emotionally. Once these triggers are recognized, individuals can take proactive steps to manage them, such as using stress-reduction techniques or communicating openly about their feelings.

Strategies for Developing Self-Awareness in Relationships

1. **Reflection**: Taking time to reflect on past interactions can help individuals gain insight into their behaviour. Journaling about conflicts or moments of emotional intensity can reveal patterns that may not be obvious in the moment. Reflection allows individuals to consider how they

reacted, what emotions were involved, and what they could have done differently.

2. **Mindfulness**: Practising mindfulness helps individuals become more present in their interactions. By focusing on the current moment without judgement, individuals can better observe their emotions and reactions. This awareness can prevent impulsive behaviours and encourage more thoughtful responses during interactions.

3. **Feedback**: Seeking feedback from trusted friends, family members, or partners can provide valuable insight into how one's behaviour is perceived by others. Constructive feedback helps individuals identify blind spots and areas for improvement, allowing them to adjust their behaviour accordingly.

4. **Emotional Regulation**: Developing the ability to manage emotions effectively is crucial for self-awareness. When individuals learn to regulate their emotions—whether it's calming

themselves during moments of anger or expressing vulnerability when feeling hurt—they are better equipped to handle the complexities of relationships.

Applying Self-Awareness to Build Healthier Relationships

Once self-awareness is developed, it becomes easier to make conscious choices that contribute to healthier relationships. For example, a person who recognizes that they often interrupt during conversations can work on listening more attentively and allowing others to speak without interruption. Similarly, someone who identifies a pattern of avoidance in conflict situations can make an effort to address issues more directly.

Incorporating self-awareness into relationships also involves being attuned to the needs and emotions of others. Empathy—understanding and sharing the feelings of another—is closely linked to self-awareness. By recognizing one's own emotional state, it becomes easier to relate to and connect with the emotions of others, leading to more compassionate and supportive behaviour.

The Role of Mental Health in Behavior

Mental health is a fundamental aspect of overall well-being, profoundly influencing behaviour, decision-making, and interpersonal relationships. Mental health challenges, such as anxiety and depression, can shape how individuals interact with their environment and respond to stressors. Understanding the interplay between mental health and behaviour is crucial for fostering healthier lifestyles and relationships.

How Anxiety, Depression, and Other Mental Health Issues Influence Behavior

Mental health conditions, including anxiety and depression, can significantly impact behaviour in various ways. These conditions can affect thought patterns, emotional responses, and the ability to function in everyday life. Individuals grappling with mental health issues often exhibit behaviours that are influenced by their emotional and psychological states.

Anxiety and Its Behavioral Impact

Anxiety is characterised by excessive worry, fear, and apprehension. It can manifest in various forms, such as generalised anxiety disorder, social anxiety disorder, or panic disorder. Individuals with anxiety often experience heightened levels of stress, which can lead to avoidance behaviours. For example, someone with social anxiety may avoid social situations altogether, fearing judgement or embarrassment. This avoidance can limit personal and professional opportunities and negatively affect relationships.

Anxiety can also lead to physical symptoms, such as restlessness, increased heart rate, or difficulty concentrating. These physical manifestations can further hinder an individual's ability to engage fully in daily activities, leading to a cycle of avoidance and increased anxiety. Additionally, anxious individuals may struggle with decision-making, often overthinking potential outcomes and fearing the worst-case scenarios.

Depression and Its Behavioral Impact

Depression, characterised by persistent feelings of sadness, hopelessness, and a lack of interest in previously enjoyable activities, can profoundly affect behaviour. Individuals with depression may withdraw from social interactions, neglect responsibilities, and experience changes in appetite and sleep patterns. This withdrawal often stems from feelings of inadequacy or the belief that others would be better off without them.

The cognitive distortions associated with depression can also influence behaviour. Individuals may view situations through a pessimistic lens, leading to feelings of helplessness and hopelessness. This distorted thinking can hinder goal-setting and motivation, making it difficult to pursue personal or professional aspirations. Consequently, individuals may become trapped in a cycle of inactivity, reinforcing their feelings of despair and inadequacy.

The Influence of Other Mental Health Issues

In addition to anxiety and depression, other mental health challenges—such as bipolar disorder, schizophrenia, or obsessive-compulsive disorder (OCD)—also impact behaviour. For instance, individuals with bipolar disorder may experience extreme mood swings, leading to impulsive decision-making during manic phases and withdrawal during depressive episodes. Similarly, those with OCD may engage in compulsive behaviours to alleviate anxiety, which can interfere with daily functioning and relationships.

Understanding the behavioural impact of various mental health issues is essential for recognizing the struggles that individuals may face. It highlights the importance of empathy and support for those grappling with these challenges, as their behaviour may often be a reflection of their internal struggles rather than a lack of effort or motivation.

Recognizing the Signs of Mental Health Challenges

Recognizing the signs of mental health challenges is a critical step toward understanding their influence on behaviour. While symptoms can vary widely among individuals, certain common indicators may suggest the presence of a mental health issue.

Common Signs of Mental Health Challenges

1. **Changes in Mood**: Frequent mood swings, irritability, or persistent sadness can signal underlying mental health issues. Individuals may experience emotional highs and lows that impact their interactions and decision-making.
2. **Withdrawal from Social Activities**: A noticeable decline in social engagement, including avoiding friends, family, or previously enjoyed activities, may

indicate that someone is struggling with their mental health. This withdrawal can lead to isolation and further exacerbate feelings of loneliness.

3. **Changes in Sleep Patterns**: Significant changes in sleep habits, such as insomnia or excessive sleeping, can be indicative of mental health challenges. Sleep disturbances can further impact emotional regulation and overall functioning.

4. **Difficulty Concentrating**: Trouble focusing, making decisions, or completing tasks can signal mental health concerns. Individuals may find themselves easily distracted or unable to engage in activities that require sustained attention.

5. **Changes in Appetite or Weight**: Noticeable changes in eating habits, whether increased or decreased appetite, can be linked to mental health issues. This can manifest as significant weight gain or loss and may also affect energy levels and mood.

6. **Physical Symptoms**: Unexplained physical symptoms, such as headaches, stomachaches, or fatigue, can often be linked to mental health issues. These symptoms may arise from the stress and emotional turmoil associated with anxiety or depression.

Recognizing these signs is crucial for individuals and their loved ones. Early identification of mental health challenges allows for timely intervention and support, which can significantly improve outcomes and prevent the exacerbation of symptoms.

Seeking Help and Support to Manage Mental Health for Better Behavior

Seeking help for mental health challenges is a vital step toward achieving better behaviour and overall well-being. It is essential to understand that mental health issues are not a sign of weakness but rather a legitimate health concern that requires attention and care.

Understanding the Importance of Help

The stigma surrounding mental health can often deter individuals from seeking the support they need. However, acknowledging the need for help is a courageous and essential step toward recovery. Professional mental health services—such as therapy, counselling, or medication—can provide individuals with the tools and resources necessary to manage their mental health effectively.

Therapy, particularly cognitive-behavioural therapy (CBT), has proven effective for many mental health conditions. CBT helps individuals identify and challenge negative thought patterns, enabling them to develop healthier behaviours and coping mechanisms. By addressing the underlying thought processes that contribute to anxiety or depression, individuals can learn to respond to stressors more positively.

In addition to professional support, building a robust support system of friends and family is crucial. Open communication with loved ones about mental health struggles fosters understanding and creates a safe space for individuals to express their feelings. Having a strong support network can help mitigate feelings of isolation and provide encouragement during challenging times.

Self-Help Strategies

While professional help is essential, individuals can also engage in self-help strategies to manage their mental health effectively. These strategies may include:

1. **Mindfulness and Meditation**: Practising mindfulness and meditation can help individuals become more aware of their thoughts and feelings, reducing anxiety and promoting emotional regulation.
2. **Physical Activity**: Regular exercise has been shown to have a positive impact on mental health. Physical activity releases endorphins, which can enhance mood and reduce stress levels.

3. **Healthy Lifestyle Choices**: Maintaining a balanced diet, getting adequate sleep, and avoiding substances like alcohol and drugs can positively affect mental health and behaviour.

4. **Setting Realistic Goals**: Establishing achievable goals can foster a sense of purpose and accomplishment, countering feelings of hopelessness associated with mental health challenges.

5. **Journaling**: Writing about thoughts and feelings can provide insight into emotions, helping individuals process their experiences and identify triggers.

Behavioral Science in Everyday Life

Behavioural science provides valuable insights into human behaviour, revealing how individuals think, feel, and act in various contexts. By applying behavioural principles to everyday situations, people can improve their interactions in work, school, and personal life. Understanding behaviour can lead to better decision-making and more effective strategies for achieving goals.

How Behavioral Principles Apply to Work, School, and Personal Life

Behavioural principles offer frameworks that can be effectively applied across various settings. In workplaces, educational institutions, and personal environments, understanding the underlying motivations and behaviours of individuals can lead to enhanced productivity, improved learning outcomes, and healthier relationships.

In the Workplace

In the workplace, behavioural science principles can enhance employee performance and foster a positive organisational culture. For example, the concept of reinforcement—rewarding desirable behaviours—can be used to increase motivation and engagement. When employees are recognized for their hard work, whether through bonuses, public acknowledgment, or opportunities for advancement, they are more likely to continue performing at high levels. This principle is rooted in B.F. Skinner's operant conditioning theory, which suggests that behaviour is shaped by its consequences.

Another relevant principle is the importance of goal setting. Clear, attainable goals help employees understand what is expected of them, and when those goals are met, individuals often feel a sense of accomplishment that boosts their confidence and productivity. Managers can implement strategies like SMART (Specific, Measurable, Achievable, Relevant, Time-bound) goals to guide their teams toward success.

Additionally, understanding workplace dynamics and group behaviour can improve collaboration. For instance, recognizing the roles individuals play within teams can enhance communication and cooperation. When team members are aware of each other's strengths and weaknesses, they can distribute tasks more effectively, leading to better outcomes.

In Educational Settings

Behavioural principles also significantly influence learning environments. In schools, educators can apply techniques derived from behavioural science to enhance student engagement and academic performance. For example, positive reinforcement—such as praise or rewards—can motivate students to participate actively in their education. When students receive recognition for their efforts, they are more likely to repeat those behaviours in the future.

Moreover, behaviour modification strategies can address classroom management issues. Techniques such as token economies—where students earn tokens for good behaviour that can be exchanged for rewards—can encourage adherence to classroom rules and enhance overall learning conditions.

Furthermore, understanding different learning styles and adapting teaching methods to accommodate diverse needs is essential. By recognizing that students may respond differently to various teaching approaches, educators can create a more inclusive environment that fosters success for all learners.

In Personal Life

In personal life, behavioural science principles can enhance relationships and promote individual well-being. Understanding the importance of communication and emotional intelligence can lead to healthier interactions. By recognizing how personal behaviours impact others and developing empathy, individuals can strengthen their relationships with friends, family, and partners.

Behavioural strategies can also help individuals make better choices regarding health and lifestyle. For instance, implementing self-monitoring techniques—such as keeping a food diary or tracking exercise—can help individuals identify patterns in their behaviour and make necessary adjustments. Similarly, setting realistic goals related to personal growth, such as improving time management or reducing stress, can lead to lasting change.

Examples of Behavior Modification in Practical Settings

Behaviour modification techniques have been successfully implemented in various practical settings, showcasing the effectiveness of behavioural science in driving positive change.

Health and Wellness

In the realm of health and wellness, behaviour modification strategies have been widely used to promote healthier lifestyles. One common example is smoking cessation programs. These programs often utilise a combination of behavioural techniques, including setting specific quit dates, identifying triggers, and providing social support. By helping individuals understand their smoking habits and the factors influencing their behaviour, these programs increase the likelihood of successful cessation.

Similarly, weight loss programs often incorporate behaviour modification principles. By encouraging participants to set achievable goals, track their progress, and receive positive reinforcement for their efforts, individuals are more likely to sustain healthy habits over the long term. Programs that focus on both dietary changes and increased physical activity tend to yield better results, as they address the multiple factors influencing weight management.

Parenting and Child Development

In parenting, behaviour modification techniques can support positive child development. Parents can employ strategies such as time-out, reward systems, and consistent consequences to guide their children's behaviour. For example, a reward chart for completing chores or homework can motivate children to take responsibility and develop good habits.

Furthermore, understanding the developmental stages of children helps parents tailor their approach to behaviour management. For instance, toddlers may benefit from simple instructions and immediate consequences, while older children can engage in discussions about their behaviour and its impact on others.

Organisational Behaviour

Behaviour modification is also prevalent in organisational behaviour. Companies often implement training programs aimed at changing employee behaviours to improve performance. For instance, safety training in manufacturing settings focuses on reinforcing safe practices and addressing risky behaviours. By utilising incentives for safe behaviour and implementing strict consequences for safety violations, organisations can cultivate a culture of safety that benefits both employees and the company as a whole.

How Understanding Behaviour Improves Decision-Making in Real-World Scenarios

Understanding behaviour plays a critical role in improving decision-making across various contexts. When individuals recognize the factors that influence their choices, they can make more informed and effective decisions.

Enhancing Personal Decision-Making

In personal decision-making, awareness of behavioural biases—such as confirmation bias, anchoring, or loss aversion—can help individuals approach choices more objectively. For example, when making a significant purchase, being aware of the tendency to favour information that supports one's existing beliefs can lead to a more balanced evaluation of options. Individuals can seek diverse perspectives and data, ultimately leading to more satisfactory outcomes.

Moreover, understanding the role of emotions in decision-making is crucial. Emotional intelligence allows individuals to recognize how their feelings influence their choices. By acknowledging emotions rather than suppressing them, individuals can make decisions that align more closely with their values and long-term goals.

In Professional Settings

In professional settings, understanding the behaviours of colleagues, clients, and stakeholders enhances decision-making processes. For instance, recognizing the importance of effective communication can improve negotiations and collaboration. When individuals understand how to tailor their communication styles to their audience, they are more likely to achieve positive outcomes.

Additionally, understanding group dynamics can facilitate better decision-making in team settings. When teams are aware of the roles and contributions of each member, they can leverage their collective strengths and minimise conflicts. This awareness fosters an environment where diverse ideas are valued, leading to more innovative solutions.

The Road to Self-Improvement: Mastering Your Behaviour

The journey of self-improvement is a lifelong commitment that involves continuous self-awareness, growth, and transformation. It encompasses not only understanding one's actions and motivations but also cultivating the ability to change and enhance one's behaviour intentionally. This chapter explains the importance of self-awareness in personal growth, the significance of self-discipline and self-control in decision-making, and the process of aligning one's life with personal values and purpose.

The Ongoing Journey of Self-Awareness and Growth

Self-awareness serves as the foundation for personal growth. It is the ability to recognize and understand one's thoughts, feelings, and behaviours. This understanding is crucial, as it provides insight into how these internal processes influence daily actions and choices. When individuals become more self-aware, they can identify patterns in their behaviour and recognize areas where improvement is needed.

One effective method for enhancing self-awareness is through regular reflection. Keeping a journal, for instance, allows individuals to articulate their thoughts and feelings, enabling them to track changes over time. This practice not only fosters clarity about one's motivations but also highlights recurring themes in behaviour, such as triggers for negative responses or patterns of procrastination.

Additionally, seeking feedback from trusted friends, family members, or colleagues can further enhance self-awareness. By inviting others to share their perspectives, individuals can gain valuable insights into how they are perceived, which may differ from their self-image. This external perspective can be instrumental in identifying blind spots and areas for growth.

Self-improvement is inherently a journey rather than a destination. It requires an ongoing commitment to learning and adapting. As individuals grow and evolve, they may encounter challenges that test their resolve. However, viewing these challenges as opportunities for growth rather than setbacks can cultivate resilience. Adopting a growth mindset—a belief that abilities and intelligence can be developed through dedication and hard work—encourages individuals to embrace challenges as part of their self-improvement journey.

Building Self-Discipline and Self-Control for Better Decision-Making

Self-discipline and self-control are essential components of effective decision-making and behaviour management. These qualities enable individuals to resist temptations, adhere to their goals, and make choices that align with their values.

Self-discipline involves the ability to set goals and consistently work towards achieving them, even when faced with distractions or challenges. It requires creating a structured environment that supports goal attainment. For instance, individuals can establish specific routines that prioritise important tasks, minimising the likelihood of procrastination. Time management techniques, such as the Pomodoro Technique, can enhance focus and productivity by breaking tasks into manageable intervals followed by short breaks.

Moreover, self-discipline is closely linked to emotional regulation. Being able to manage one's emotions in high-pressure situations is crucial for maintaining focus on long-term goals. Techniques such as deep breathing, mindfulness meditation, or even physical exercise can help individuals regulate their emotions and cultivate a sense of calm, making it easier to resist impulsive behaviours.

Self-control, on the other hand, refers to the ability to suppress short-term desires in favour of long-term benefits. It is often tested in situations where immediate gratification is appealing, such as indulging in unhealthy foods or procrastinating on important tasks. Strategies for enhancing self-control include creating barriers to temptation, such as avoiding environments that trigger impulsive behaviour. For instance, individuals aiming to eat healthier may choose to avoid fast-food restaurants or keep unhealthy snacks out of the house.

Another effective approach is to practise delayed gratification. When faced with an impulse, individuals can train themselves to wait for a predetermined period before acting on that impulse. This practice reinforces self-control by allowing time for reflection and consideration of long-term consequences.

Creating a Life Aligned with Your Values and Purpose

Creating a life that aligns with one's values and purpose is a crucial aspect of self-improvement. When individuals are clear about their values—what truly matters to them—they can make decisions that reflect those principles, leading to a more fulfilling and meaningful life.

To begin this process, individuals can start by identifying their core values. This can be done through self-reflection or by using value assessment tools. Once individuals have a clear understanding of their values, they can evaluate their current behaviours and decisions against these principles. This evaluation process may reveal discrepancies between what individuals claim to value and how they spend their time and energy.

For instance, someone who values health may find themselves neglecting exercise in favour of work or leisure activities. Recognizing this misalignment provides an opportunity for change. By prioritising activities that reflect their values, individuals can cultivate a greater sense of satisfaction and purpose in their lives.

Setting specific, value-driven goals can further reinforce alignment. These goals should be meaningful and directly related to one's core values. For example, if family is a core value, setting a goal to spend more quality time with loved ones can lead to enhanced relationships and personal fulfilment. When goals are in harmony with one's values, individuals are more likely to feel motivated and committed to pursuing them.

Moreover, aligning one's life with purpose involves a commitment to continuous growth and adaptation. As individuals navigate their journey of self-improvement, they may find that their values and priorities evolve. Being open to this evolution and willing to adjust goals accordingly ensures that individuals remain aligned with their true selves.

Conclusion: The Path to Behavioral Mastery

The journey toward behavioural mastery is both complex and rewarding, offering profound insights into the nature of human behaviour and the factors that shape it. Throughout this exploration, we have examined the various elements influencing our actions, from motivation and relationships to mental health and self-awareness. As we reflect on these insights, it becomes clear that understanding our behaviour is not merely an academic exercise; it is a vital component of personal growth and transformation.

Reflecting on the Insights Gained

One of the most significant insights gained from this exploration is the intricate interplay between our thoughts, emotions, and behaviours. Recognizing that our actions are influenced by a variety of internal and external factors enables us to take a more holistic approach to self-improvement. This understanding lays the foundation for meaningful change, as it encourages us to look beyond surface-level behaviours and examine the underlying motivations and beliefs that drive them.

Moreover, the realisation that behaviour is not fixed but rather a dynamic process allows for greater flexibility in our personal growth journey. By adopting a mindset that embraces change and development, we can view setbacks not as failures but as opportunities for learning and growth. This perspective fosters resilience, enabling us to navigate challenges with a greater sense of purpose and determination.

The importance of relationships in shaping behaviour also cannot be overstated. The connections we form with others—whether intimate or social—play a critical role in influencing our actions and decisions. Understanding this interconnectedness encourages us to cultivate healthier relationships and improve our communication skills, thereby enhancing our capacity for empathy and compassion. As we build stronger bonds with others, we create an environment that supports our behavioural growth and fosters a sense of belonging.

Encouraging Ongoing Self-Reflection and Commitment to Personal Growth

As we conclude this exploration, it is essential to emphasise the importance of ongoing self-reflection. This practice not only deepens our understanding of ourselves but also enables us to identify areas for improvement and set meaningful goals. Regularly engaging in self-reflection helps us maintain clarity about our values, aspirations, and the behaviours we wish to cultivate.

To support this process, individuals can develop a routine that includes moments of introspection, whether through journaling, meditation, or simply taking time to think. By establishing these habits, we create a foundation for continuous growth and self-discovery. Additionally, seeking feedback from trusted individuals can provide valuable insights and perspectives, further enhancing our understanding of ourselves.

Commitment to personal growth requires a willingness to embrace change and face challenges head-on. It is crucial to recognize that the path to behavioural mastery is not linear; it is filled with ups and downs. Embracing this reality fosters a sense of perseverance and encourages individuals to stay committed to their growth journey, even when faced with obstacles.

Final Thoughts on the Importance of Understanding Why You Behave the Way You Do

Understanding the reasons behind our behaviours is fundamental to achieving lasting change. By examining the motivations, beliefs, and emotional triggers that drive our actions, we empower ourselves to make informed choices. This awareness serves as a catalyst for personal growth, allowing us to break free from unhelpful patterns and create a life aligned with our values and aspirations.

Furthermore, this understanding extends beyond the individual; it enhances our relationships with others. When we recognize the complexities of human behaviour, we can approach interactions with greater empathy and understanding. This not only improves our communication skills but also fosters a sense of connection and collaboration, enriching our social interactions.

In closing, the journey toward behavioural mastery is a continuous process that requires dedication, self-reflection, and a willingness to learn. By embracing the insights gained throughout this exploration, individuals can take meaningful steps toward understanding their behaviour and, ultimately, achieving personal growth. As we navigate the complexities of our lives, let us remain committed to this journey, recognizing that the path to mastery is as important as the destination itself. Each step taken in self-discovery and behavioural understanding brings us closer to becoming the individuals we aspire to be.